TAKING BACK THE CLASSROOM:
TIPS FOR THE COLLEGE
PROFESSOR ON BECOMING A
MORE EFFECTIVE TEACHER

Delaney J. Kirk, Ph.D.

FOREWARD

Both new and experienced faculty members are wondering how to manage today's college students. That is why *Taking Back the Classroom: Tips for the College Professor on Becoming a More Effective Teacher* is a must read for all college professors. It is a proactive primer on classroom management in higher education for the 21st Century.

The book is developed from a series of workshops on classroom management conducted by Dr. Delaney J. Kirk over many years. It provides a 240-page toolbox filled with proven classroom management techniques that have been used successfully by faculty in all disciplines.

Taking Back the Classroom is divided into 12 chapters, each focusing on key issues such as what to do on the first day of class to establish your credibility, how to handle difficult and challenging students, and legal advice on sexual harassment in the classroom. By adhering to Dr. Kirk's advice, as well as suggestions from her colleagues and former workshop participants, college faculty can aggressively take charge of the classroom to create the best learning environments for their students.

---Geralyn McClure Franklin, Ph.D.
Dean, School of Business
University of Texas of the Permian Basin
July 2005

ACKNOWLEDGEMENTS

*Life is ten percent what happens to me
and ninety percent how I react to it.*
---Charles Swindoll

I would like to thank Laura McVay, Doug Grider, and Lisa Boomershine for their willingness to read my manuscript at an early stage and their encouragement to keep going. Special thanks especially goes to Nancy Leonard, West Virginia University, and Paula Thonney, Brookdale Community College, for their many organizational suggestions—their footprints are all over this book.

Thanks to Brad Meyer for writing the chapter on Managing Online Classes based on his decade of experience in teaching web-based courses. His suggestions make the idea of teaching online courses much less scary.

I especially want to thank my editor, Aaron Peden, at Tiberius Publications for his support when I felt overwhelmed by this project, his great suggestions for organizing and editing the book, and his ability to keep smiling throughout the process.

And lastly, I have to acknowledge my "Class from Hell" which made me re-examine how I presented myself and managed my classroom. I can truly say I am in charge and enjoying teaching again.

CONTENTS IN BRIEF

CONTENTS

INTRODUCTION

Why Read This Book?

Teaching is a performing art with content.
                                    ---**Anonymous**

Is it just me or do college students seem to lack respect for their professors today? Have students become more demanding, less responsible, and deficient in plain old common courtesy? What ever happened to civility in the classroom? Interestingly enough, Albert Shanker, former president of the American Federation of Teachers, addressed this potential problem as far back as 1995.[1] He stated that kids misbehave in public schools because the students have been "taught" that this is acceptable at an early age. A six-year-old child is disruptive and the other children look around to see what will happen. The kids are convinced that if a lightening bolt does not come down from the sky, that at the very least the student will be sent to the principal's office. But, as Shanker says, many times nothing happens. There is no punishment. The rest of the students realize that the teacher is not the leader... the six-year-old kid is.

Fast forward twelve years and these same students are now in college. My first introduction to this problem of classroom management occurred a few years ago when I experienced the "Class from Hell." At the time I had been teaching for over 20 years and was just dumbfounded by the behavior of the students in this class. They came to class late, their cell phones rang during the lecture, and they left in the middle of class to go to the rest room. One student even fell asleep during every class period. I got to the point where I hated to go into that classroom. I found myself obsessing over my lack of control, getting angrier and angrier with those "stupid, bad, disrespectful students." I whined to my colleagues and seriously thought about leaving teaching for something, anything else... I finally decided I had to do something for my own sanity, if not my career.

> *I told my botany class that I would not tolerate cell phones ringing and disturbing the final, and a student asked, "Why do you have to be so stupid?"*
> **---Jennith Maclean Thomas**
> **Louisburg College**

I decided to return to a "zero tolerance" policy for disruptive behavior. I went back into my "Class from Hell" at mid-term and laid down some new ground rules. First, I apologized. I explained that I had not been a good manager of the classroom. I had not established and communicated my expectations to them. I had no right to be angry when they did not do what I wanted. So I told the students...here are the rules for the rest of the semester.

I have to admit that even I, a tenured full professor, hesitated before laying down the law with that class. After all, those all-important teaching evaluations are used in making my pay raise decisions too. However, as I found out by talking to friends and colleagues at other universities, we are all struggling with the same issues. While most of us are comfortable with the content of what we are teaching, many of us do not believe that our doctorate-granting institutions have prepared us in the "how-to's" of managing our classrooms. Even those of us who have been teaching for a while may not think that we really know how to handle disruptive behaviors from our students. In fact, we believe we shouldn't have to; after all, shouldn't college students know how to conduct themselves in a classroom?

> *An associate anthropology professor at the University of Nebraska had two students start making out in her classroom during her lecture one day. She had to ask them to leave.*[2]
> ---**Jenna Johnson**
> **Daily Nebraskan**

Why are we having so much trouble with our students? Part of this is probably our own fault as instructors. Many of my colleagues "dress down" to go to class and have the students call them by their first name as a way to relate. We want our students to like us. In addition, universities are putting an emphasis on the student as customer and giving teaching evaluations a great deal of weight in determining renewals of contracts. Thus, my colleagues tell me they are afraid to say no when asked to allow late papers, give extra credit, or make-up tests. They feel they have lost control of their own classrooms.

> *A colleague of mine was having a lot of trouble with her students. She asked me to sit in on one of her classes and give her some feedback. I was in the back of the room the next day when she came in and started to lecture. One of her students piped up and announced that class didn't start for another two minutes, and my colleague stopped and waited. Even the students knew that she had lost control of that class.*
>
> **---Dr. Kirk**

Learning to manage your classroom is a craft that can be learned and improved upon like any other skill. This book presents suggestions based on my own experiences, those of colleagues at other universities, and ideas from participants in my workshops on classroom management. You are not alone. We all want to do a better job of teaching in an environment conducive to learning.

And what about the class that inspired this book? Did the students "ding" me on evaluations at the end of that semester? No. In fact, they seemed appreciative that I had established some guidelines and enforced these fairly. Perhaps in the long run they find this new informality in the classroom uncomfortable as well.

I had the temerity to suggest to my Dean that it might be useful for our faculty to develop strategies for classroom management. As a fresh-faced, untenured assistant professor who had no training in teaching prior to entering academe, I had been subjected to various forms of rude behavior and disrespect by students. Many of these students apparently felt no compunction about acting out in class, as I assume they probably did in high school. My Dean instantly dismissed my recommendation and suggested I just hunker down and get with the program! "It is your class – manage it!" I reached my breaking point in 2004 when a student had the audacity to take a cell phone call during my lecture. I completely retooled my syllabi to include my expectations of the students, setting clear boundaries of acceptable and unacceptable behaviors. I also articulate expectations of myself – that is, what students should expect from me including maintaining generous office hours, treating them with dignity and respect, and responding promptly to email and telephone inquiries. More importantly, I use the entire first class lecture to go through the fine details of the syllabus. Setting clear expectations has resulted in a more productive and engaging classroom environment and has helped defuse potential crisis situations. Just as parents model behavior for their children, so do we, as professors, have to model behavior for our students.

---James Montgomery
DePaul University

How the Book is Organized

Taking Back the Classroom was developed from questions and issues raised at workshops on classroom management that I have been teaching for a number of years.

The Book Contains:
- Examples and tips based on my 25 years of teaching at the college level.

- Suggestions and "war stories" from faculty at a number of colleges and universities.

- Sample forms, rubrics, and contracts that you can adapt for use in your own classroom.

- Specific questions and answers on class management topics in the Questions from Faculty sections.

- Unique student perspectives as to what makes for good or bad teaching in the Comments from Students sections. These students represent a variety of majors from a large public university, a small private college, and a two-year community college.

Where to Start?

Are you a new instructor trying to decide what you need to tell your students about your expectations in the classroom? Chapters 1 and 2 provide suggestions for choosing your classroom policies and communicating these in your syllabus.

Are you struggling with how to manage the new generation of college students? Chapters 3 and 4 discuss the importance of first impressions in order to create the class culture you want. Both new and experienced faculty should consider how they establish their credibility and make a connection with their students on that crucial first day of contact.

Do you have students who come to you for advice on sexual harassment incidents? Are you concerned about protecting yourself from sexual harassment accusations? Chapter 5 contains both legal advice and counseling suggestions.

Are there students in your class with physical or learning disabilities and you are not sure what your responsibilities are for accommodating them? Do you have international students that you cannot seem to understand or connect with? Is there a wide range of ages in your class and you are not sure how to motivate everyone? Chapter 6 presents suggestions on how to engage all your students in the classroom.

Do you have students who come to class late, dominate the discussions, leave in the middle of class, or engage in other types of disruptive behaviors? Chapter 7 examines a wide range of inappropriate classroom behaviors and makes suggestions for addressing these with the goal of fostering an ideal classroom environment.

Are you struggling with exam issues such as makeup policies, cheating, and requests for extra credit? Would you like to create learning opportunities for students without just giving them points? See Chapter 8 for ideas.

Would you like to use team projects in your class but need advice on how to assign teams, how to build team skills, how to evaluate team participation, and how to handle complaints about team members? Chapter 9 addresses these issues.

Are you teaching a large class and want suggestions on how to handle issues of attendance, tardiness, participation, and getting feedback? Chapter 10 looks at how professors of large classes can still build a relationship with their students.

Has your university asked you to teach an online course and you want to know how to set class expectations, facilitate forum discussions, manage online exams, make a connection between you and the students, and manage the time demands of the class? See Chapter 11 for advice from Dr. Bradley Meyer who has been teaching online classes since 1996.

And finally, would you like some tips for teaching accumulated from over 25 years of teaching experience at the college level? Chapter 12 presents suggestions on how to become a more effective teacher.

Take Back Your Classroom and Become A More Effective Teacher!

Endnotes:

[1]Shanker, Albert, "Classrooms Held Hostage," *American Educator*, Vol 19(1), 1995.

[2]Johnson, Jenna, "Drake Professor Addresses Classroom Behavior in New Book," *Daily Nebraskan*, September 24, 2004.

CHAPTER 1

Determining Classroom Policies

*A teacher affects eternity; he can never
tell where his influence stops.*
---Henry B. Adams

Until you encounter that one student who drives
you nuts with his or her behavior, you may
not realize what expectations you have of your
classroom. However, you cannot be an effective
teacher until you decide on these expectations,
communicate them to your students, and then
enforce the rules fairly and consistently.

Determining your policies requires reflection on
what you think is the ideal classroom environment. You will have to decide if attendance is
important to you, if you need to have a policy on
late papers, or if bringing food or wearing hats
in the classroom is disruptive behavior. Each
professor has different tolerances and you need
to concentrate on what you think is important in
order to create a learning environment. It might
be helpful to talk to your colleagues about the
expectations and policies they have for their students. You could also look back on some of your
less-than-ideal student experiences and identify
what you could have done in order to prevent
those problems. Your university will have a stu-

dent handbook that addresses some behavioral issues for you. Citing this "official" handbook will lend more weight to your policies on issues such as cheating, sexual harassment, and showing respect in the classroom.

It is important to have a rationale for your policies. Keep in mind that you are role modeling successful behavior of the "real world" for your students. Coming to class is important so that the latecomers do not disrupt the learning for others. Turning in assignments on time is part of learning to be responsible and practicing good time management skills that will then serve the students well in their workplaces. You are not being arbitrary and dictatorial. You are being fair and reasonable and helping the students to be successful in their current roles as students as well as in their future careers as professionals. You will find that most students will obey your policies if you spell out what they are and why they are important.

As you think through your policies, keep in mind that each one needs to be:

- Clearly written in your syllabus
- Communicated orally the first day of class
- Have a rationale so the policy is seen as reasonable
- Have consequences for students who do not follow the policy
- Be enforced consistently

Some professors develop a list of what their students can expect from them as well as a set of classroom rules for the students. Professor Laura Ginger at Indiana University shares her expectations for herself in Figure 1.1 and for her students in Figure 1.2 at the end of this chapter.

The following are items that you may want to address in your classroom policies.

Attendance Policy
Explain to your students why you think attendance is important if that is the case. Some professors do not keep track of attendance as they believe the students, or their parents, have paid for the course; if they do not want to attend, that is their choice. They also think that tracking attendance takes away from valuable class time especially in a large class.

Most professors believe it is important to encourage students to attend class because at some point, they will have to go to work on a regular basis and on time. In addition, research shows a correlation between attendance and successful performance in classes.[1] If class size is the problem, Chapter 10 gives some suggestions on encouraging attendance in larger classes.

Wording I have used in my policy on attendance is: "Attendance in class is very important as numerous experiential exercises, cases, guest speakers, and presentations will be used to illustrate various methods of managing employees. Excessive absences will have an adverse effect on a student's final grade. More than two absences will be considered excessive and will result in loss of participation points."

---Dr. Kirk

Tardiness Policy

Tell your students that you expect them to be in class, seated, and ready to participate at the beginning of the class. Instruct them that if they do come in late, they should enter the room quietly and sit close to the door. If you take attendance at the beginning of class, you could require those who are late to see you after class so you can correct your attendance sheet. Following this policy should deter most of the students and also give you a chance to speak to any tardy students about your attendance expectations. Chapter 7 on Managing Difficult Students includes suggestions for dealing with habitual offenders of your policies for attendance and tardiness.

Expectations During Class

If allowed, students will get up in the middle of class to do everything from making phone calls to going to the rest room. This is disruptive to the professor as well as to other students in the classroom. One method of solving this problem would be to tell your students that they are expected to spend the entire time in class. Any exceptions to this rule should be approved by you prior to the class period.

> *Students will always be springing things on you that you NEVER in your wildest dreams expected to have happen in the classroom. I had a student in my class one day that was chewing tobacco and spitting it out in a clear water bottle. I realize that substance addictions enslave people and that merely chewing out (pardon the pun) the student was just going to alienate him. I took him aside, treated him with respect, and calmly told him that I didn't think it was appropriate to 'do that' in class. I could tell by his body language that he expected me to be disgusted with him or express revulsion at such a nasty habit. I could have, but I didn't. I could tell he was really grateful that I didn't embarrass him or put him down, and he never brought his 'stuff' to class again. Actually his attitude improved remarkably after that day.*
>
> **---Paula Thonney,**
> **Brookdale Community College**

Participation in Class

One of the things you will need to decide is whether you expect your students to actively participate during the class and if you want to give them points for this. Determining how to grade participation can be a challenge but the act of participating moves the students from passive spectators to active partners in the learning process. Giving credit for participation allows you discretionary points that you can use to reward students for complying with your classroom rules. You could use a seating chart and put a check mark next to the names of students who make insightful comments and questions.

Food and Drink in the Classroom

You will need a policy on students eating and drinking during class if you think this is disruptive. Check to see if your university has a campus policy against food and drink in the classrooms. If you decide to allow food and beverages, address the issue of having respect for your classmates by not bringing in loud or smelly food items. Also, emphasize that the students need to clean up after themselves when they leave.

Cell Phones, Pagers, and Computers

A relatively new problem is the technology that students bring into the class. In a survey done at the University of Arizona, 79 percent of the students listed cell phones and beepers as the biggest distractions in the classroom.[2] You will need to remind your students to turn off, or silence, their cell phones and pagers before class.

> *Inevitably a student's phone will ring during class the first week or so. I like to stop my lecture, look at the student directly, and say with a smile, "That better be for me." The students laugh but are then more diligent about turning their phones off before class.*
>
> **---Dr. Kirk**

An increasing number of universities are bundling laptops into tuition fees and are encouraging students to take their computers to class. This leads to students surfing the net, playing computer games, and sending answers to assignments back and forth. You will have to emphasize that if students are using a laptop computer, it is to be used for taking notes or class-related work only. However, enforcing this rule may be a challenge; making the lectures interesting and requiring the students to actively participate will help.

> *Issues with laptops have soared on campuses with wireless setups. I recently became aware that we have students out in the hall who are instant messaging the kids in the class. They're carrying on completely separate realities when it looks like they're taking notes!*
>
> **---Nancy Leonard,**
> **West Virginia University**

Late Papers and Assignments

You will need to decide if you will accept late papers and if you will deduct points for these. You may want to have a separate policy that you do not accept late homework or short papers that are not worth many points. Allow students to miss a couple of these without penalty. With major assignments, consider deducting points for each day late. Set a final deadline past which you will not accept the assignment. Explain to the students that it is not fair to other students in the class that they have extra time to complete their papers and that is why you deduct points.

Cheating and Plagiarism

Your university will have a policy that deals with cheating and plagiarism. You can either cut and paste that into your syllabus or refer to the policy in the student handbook or university website. This conveys to the students that it is not just your policy, but that of the university. As an employee of the university you are in a position of responsibility to enforce the school's rules and have no option but to take suitable action if a student is found cheating. Include a definition of cheating and plagiarism. Some students seem to be unclear about what constitutes academic dishonesty so examples are helpful. Chapter 7 on Managing Difficult Students and Chapter 8 on Managing Exams present specific ways of preventing cheating on papers and exams.

> *Years ago I had a student turn in a paper where he actually plagiarized an article that I had published the year before! I kept thinking as I read his paper that this sounds familiar....*
> **---Dr. Kirk**

Respect in the Classroom

You may want to discuss what kinds of actions are indicative of respectful students, such as being prepared for class, listening attentively, and not interrupting while the professor or others are talking. You should also address disrespectful behaviors such as talking to classmates during lecture, reading newspapers or books, working on materials for other classes, or sleeping in class. Include a statement on respecting others. Many universities will have a general anti-

harassment policy for the student body that prohibits negative comments and behaviors based
on race, gender, national origin, disability, and
religion. You can refer to the student handbook
for wording on anti-harassment policies.

Indicate the consequences for disruptive or harassing behavior such as the loss of participation points or being asked to leave the class.

> *I include the statement, "Students are expected
> to keep an open mind and treat members of the
> class, guest speakers, and me with respect"
> on my syllabus.*
>
> **---Dr. Kirk**

Communicate Your Classroom Policies
Regardless of what policies you decide to have
for your class, it is important to communicate
these to your students. Chapter 4 on Managing
the First Day of Class will present ways to help
you do this.

A method of getting the students to "buy into"
your classroom policies is to require them to keep
a daily grade certification form. Professor Charles
E. Cardwell at Pellissippi State Technical Community College developed the form in Figure 1.3.
Students in his philosophy class keep track of
their own attendance, arrival, preparation, and
participation each day. Professor Cardwell says
it takes only a few minutes after class to record
the grade to his grade sheet. He believes that
the process of filling out the form encourages his
students to be more engaged in the class.

A Final Note

As mentioned earlier, you will find that the students will follow your classroom policies if they make sense to the students and they know what your expectations are. This chapter presented behavioral issues you should address both orally and in your syllabus. However, you will not be able to anticipate all the types of behaviors that will be disruptive in your classroom.

Deal with behaviors you do not like right away. If a student breaks a rule, handle it quickly and consistently by pulling the student aside after class and reminding him or her of the class policy. If you do not address issues immediately, the student will continue to break the rules. Remember that the other students in class are watching to see if and how you enforce your own classroom policies. Specific examples of rule breakers and how to handle various situations are discussed in detail in Chapter 7.

I didn't realize until my "Class from Hell" how much I wanted and expected my students to stay for the entire class period. I would put them into groups to work on a class assignment and several students would get up and leave the room for a cigarette or restroom break. The rest of their group would have to wait for them to come back in order to complete their task. Other issues during class such as text-messaging on a cell phone or playing games on a laptop I would never have anticipated when I first starting teaching.

---Dr. Kirk

Figure 1.1: What You Can Expect From Your Professor

1. I will be fully prepared for class and will be ready to start the class on time. This includes having all handouts and blackboard material available before class starts.
2. I will end the class on time or within two minutes of the scheduled ending time.
3. I will stick to the syllabus schedule and topics as closely as possible.
4. I will do my part to make sure class time is valuable to the students who attend.
5. I will abide by the grading scale, course policies, exam dates, etc. listed in the syllabus and will not change these in the middle of the semester.
6. I will answer e-mail questions from students thoroughly and within twelve hours or less.
7. I will listen to in-class questions from students carefully and will answer them thoroughly. If I do not know the answer, I will find it out and report back.
8. I will grade student quizzes and exams and return these to the students promptly-this means no later than the next class period.
9. I will be available during my scheduled office hours. If I must change office hours on a particular day, I will notify students in advance by e-mail (and in class if possible).
10. I will be civil and professional in my dealings with students.

Figure 1.2: What I Expect From My Students

1. Students will arrive for class and be in their seats and ready to begin on time.
2. Students who arrive late will find a seat as close to the door as possible and sit down quickly and quietly.
3. Students who arrive late to a quiz will sit down quietly so as not to disrupt students who are working on the quiz. They will wait until class is over to ask for a copy of the quiz, and will not ask to make it up.
4. Students will stay until the end of class, and will not pack up before that time.
5. Students who have to arrive late or leave early for a compelling reason on a particular day will inform me of that fact in advance.
6. Students will not leave during class and come back unless they have a medical emergency such as a nosebleed, vomiting, diarrhea, etc. Students who have chronic medical conditions which may require them to leave and come back must inform me of that fact at the beginning of the semester, and must sit near the door.
7. Students will take care of their needs for the rest room, coffee, returning phone calls, etc. before class begins so they can stay and pay attention for the entire class period.
8. Students will turn off all ringers on cell phones, pagers, and other devices during class.

Figure 1.2 Continued:

9. Students will pay attention during class: no talking while classmates or I am talking, no sleeping, no reading newspapers, no doing work for other classes. Students who are asked to leave for the day for engaging in these behaviors will do so quickly and quietly.

10. Students will address me respectfully in person and in e-mail.

11. Students will not e-mail me to ask questions which are answered in the syllabus.

12. Students will keep in mind that the course rules and policies, exam dates, and grading scale apply to all students equally, and will not ask for special treatment.

13. Students who miss class will get the lecture notes from another student and will pick up any handouts they missed. They will not ask me to give them notes or repeat an entire lecture just for them.

14. Students who have questions during class will raise their hands and wait to be called on.

15. Students will conduct themselves with personal integrity and honesty. They will carefully read and follow the Honor Code of the School of Business.

Source: Laura Ginger, Indiana University

Figure 1.3: Daily
Grade Certification Form

Date _____

By circling the scores below, I, _____
hereby solemnly declare and affirm that:

Attendance: circle the scores for ALL that apply
I came to class:	1
I arrived on time:	1
I stayed in class the full class period:	1

Preparation: circle the ONE score that best applies
I didn't read the assignment before class:	0
I scanned the assignment quickly before class:	1
I studied the assignment carefully before class:	2

Participation: circle the ONE or TWO scores that apply
I didn't pay much attention to class discussion:	0
I listened attentively to the class discussion:	1
I contributed to class discussion:	1

Add the circled scores for your
DAILY GRADE: _____

**Source: Charles E. Cardwell, Pellissippi
State Technical Community College**

Questions from Faculty

Dear Dr. Kirk:
You talk about "setting expectations for acceptable behavior" on the first day of class. How do you not scare students away while doing this?
Need Students in Order to Teach

Dear Need Students,
Hmm... scaring them into behaving well is a bad thing? Seriously, I find that most students will follow your policies if they see them as reasonable and you don't play favorites in enforcing them. I tell them that when they get a job after college, it would be useful to know their manager's expectations. I'm just telling them how to be successful in my workplace, the classroom.

Dear Dr. Kirk:
What should I do about students who use politically incorrect or vulgar terms in the classroom? They don't seem to blink at these expressions, but I find it inappropriate.
I'm Really Not a Fuddy-duddy

Dear Not a Fuddy-duddy,
Part of the problem is that students are so used to hearing vulgar language from their friends, movies, music, etc. I think you have to make them aware that this is not appropriate in the work world. Recently, one of my students referred to a female classmate as a "chick." I turned to him and jokingly said I was not aware that we had farm animals in the classroom. Everyone laughed, but they got my point.

Comments from Students

My best professors let me know what was going on in the class at the start of the semester, kept pretty close to schedule, were clear about their expectations, and made class interesting.

Mary

The best professors I've had were respectful and you could tell they really cared about what the students learned and how well their students were doing in the class. They were very professional in class settings and it made students want to go to class.

Ned

I had a professor who did not follow the syllabus, and awarded "extra" points arbitrarily. I guess basically what I am saying is I enjoy a structured classroom, not necessarily ruling with an iron fist, but staying on task.

Tim

My worst professor taught journalism. He was disorganized, condescending, and unable to adapt to the dynamics in the classroom.

Megan

Endnotes:

[1]Romer, David, "Do Students Go to Class? Should They?" *The Journal of Economic Perspectives*, Summer 1993; Schmidt, Robert M., "Who Maximizes What? A Study in Student Time Allocation," *American Economic Review*, May 1983; Park, Kang H. and Peter M. Kerr, "Determinants of Academic Performance: A Multinomial Logit Approach," *The Journal of Economic Education*, Spring 1990.

[2]Young, Jeffrey R., "Sssshhh. We're Taking Notes Here: Colleges Look for New Ways to Discourage Disruptive Behavior in the Classroom," *Chronicle of Higher Education*, August 8, 2003.

CHAPTER 2

Writing An Effective Syllabus

Would you tell me, please,
which way I ought to go from here?
That depends a good deal
on where you want to get to.
---Lewis Carroll

An effective syllabus is essentially a map that shows the students how to proceed successfully from the first to the final day of class. It also is similar to an employee handbook as it is a source for the day-to-day questions that the students have regarding classroom policies and expectations. The syllabus helps the professor plan the course before the class even meets.

If a schedule is included, both students and the professor understand what they need to do each day. Another perk of the syllabus is that it indicates to the students that the professor is organized and has thoroughly planned the class.

Most universities do not have set expectations for a syllabus except to note that each professor should probably have one. You should check to see if there is a required format in your school. If not, you might ask your colleagues if they would share their syllabi with you.

Think about what a student needs to know about your class on the first day. Also, consider what policies you should have in writing so that there are no unpleasant surprises later for the student.

> *I have a policy manual instead of a syllabus. Each semester students turn in comments and advice for the next semester's class. They include their name and then I use some of these in the manual for the next class. I find that students are more willing to listen to other students than they are to me as to how to be successful in my class.*
>
> **---Tim Peterson**
> **Oklahoma State University**

The following are typical components of an effective syllabus. There is also a sample syllabus in the Appendix.

Basic Information
The basic information that students need to know about your course including:

- Name and course number of class
- Prerequisites of the class
- Professor's name
- Location of professor's office
- Office hours
- Office phone number
- E-mail address of professor
- Web site address, if you have one

Also, include what students should do if they need to see you outside office hours. If you have teaching assistants, include their names, phone numbers, and office hours. If the class has a lab, include the location of the lab, and days and times that the lab meets.

Some professors give their students their home phone number. However, you can be readily available to your students through answering machines and e-mail so this is probably not necessary. If you do give out your home number, be sure and note restrictions on your syllabus such as, "Please respect my home life by not calling this number after 10:00pm or before 8:00am."

Textbook and Materials
Provide the students with a list of textbooks, supplemental workbooks, and lab materials. Be sure and indicate whether the books are optional or required for class. Many students are now buying their textbooks online so include publisher, edition, and ISBN numbers. You might consider e-mailing your list of textbooks to your students a few weeks before class begins so that they have time to order the books. Textbooks have become very expensive so if you require books, you need to be sure and use them extensively.

Include in this section any materials such as required calculators, computer software, art supplies, and lab equipment.

Brief Course Description
Include the course description that is in your university's course catalog. However, if the description of your course has been updated since the catalog was published, incorporate the more current information.

Learning Objectives
Here you might include five to seven main objectives of the class to help the students understand your expectations.

In their book, *Learner-Centered Assessment on College Campuses: Shifting the Focus From Teaching to Learning*, Mary Huba and Jann Freed suggest thinking through two questions in planning your course objectives.[1]

• What will your students know after the class is over that they didn't know before?

• What will they be able to do with this new knowledge?

Techniques of Instruction
Tell your students how they will be spending their class time. Indicate the percentage of time you will be lecturing, working on team projects, watching videos, discussing cases, completing experiential exercises, reviewing journal articles, and conducting class discussion. A variety of teaching methods will make the class more interesting to your students.

Examinations
Indicate the number of exams, what they will cover, and whether the final is comprehensive. Include a statement to the students that it is important that they take the exams at the assigned time. However, in those cases where this is not possible, inform your students your policy on makeup exams. Chapter 8 on Managing Exams includes some sample policies.

Determining Grades
Indicate your grading scale in the class (90-100% is a "A," 80-89% is a "B" and so forth). Also, show how final grades will be determined, including the total number of points available and the number of points allocated for tests, projects, papers, or labs. If you are teaching undergraduate students, you will want to have enough points that students feel they can miss some and still do well in the class. Use points instead of letter grades for individual assignments and tests.

Major Assignments
List the major papers, projects, and other work that will be assigned. Provide enough information about these assignments so students can get an idea of what they will be doing for the class. Students look at this section very carefully to determine workload expectations.

Attendance
You may want a separate section on attendance if you take attendance and use it in your final grading. Explain why attending class is important to you and to your students' success in

the class. Tell your students if you want them to contact you beforehand if they have to miss class.

Class Participation

Indicate whether active participation in class is expected and how this will be graded. Obviously with larger classes this may be more difficult. Some professors grade participation by counting attendance with the thought that if the students do not come to class, they are obviously not participating.

> *Every lecture I draw a vertical line on the board that is 12 inches long with short tick marks up and down its length. At the top of the line I print, "very difficult," the bottom, "very easy" and the middle, "average." I call this the "TESTOM-ETER." I then put a large dot on the "average" tick mark. I tell my students, "OK, I love questions. If you do not ask me any, I will assume you all understand the lecture completely, so I can make the next exam harder." I then move the dot up a notch. There is an immediate undercurrent of angst, with students telling their friends to "Ask a question!" If I begin to get some good questions, I lower the dot, again stating that I must be doing a lousy job explaining this concept, so I'd better make the test easier. After a while, all I have to do is start walking over to the TESTOMETER and hands go up.*
>
> ---**Dave Bloomquist**
> **University of Florida**

Disabilities and Religious Considerations
Ask students to indicate within the first two weeks whether they will need any special considerations due to disabilities or religious holidays. Your university will have a formal process for students to request reasonable accommodations related to disabilities. See Chapter 6 for a discussion of types of disabilities and suggestions on how to help these students be successful in the classroom.

Academic Dishonesty
Copy, word for word, your university's policy on cheating and plagiarism and include it in your syllabus. Be sure to discuss this in class as well. Many students do not understand what constitutes plagiarism or the importance of citing the work of others.

Support Services Available
On your syllabus, include library resources, computer labs, web sites, relevant journals, tutoring services, learning centers, and other resources available to the student at your university.

Classroom Policies and Expectations
Include all of the classroom policies you have developed as discussed in Chapter 1 such as attendance, tardiness, cell phones, cheating, late assignments, and leaving the classroom early.

Tips for Success
Consider adding a few tips for success for your students. Put in suggestions for time management, study skills, and test-taking. You might

also add a few sample quiz or exam questions with answers. Ron Theys at the University of Wisconsin-Fond du Lac shares some of his study tips for his chemistry students in Figure 2.1.

Frequently Asked Questions (FAQs)

In addition, you might include questions and answers about assignments, exams, class expectations, etc., that students tend to ask. Paula Thonney at Brookdale Community College does this for her students in her algebra classes. See Figure 2.2 for examples of FAQs she includes on her syllabus.

Schedule for Classes

Listing a schedule for the class is optional, but once done it will make the class easier to keep organized. This is usually put at the end of the syllabus. Be sure and note that the schedule is tentative and thus subject to change as the class progresses. Try to put down what chapters or modules you plan to cover each day or each week, when tests will be scheduled, when major assignments are due, etc. To help you and your students with planning for the semester, tell them that you will not change dates of tests or major assignments so they can go ahead and put these on their calendar. You will find this helps lessen the number of makeup exams.

Quiz on the Syllabus

In order to emphasize the importance of reading and understanding your syllabus, give the students a short quiz on it the second week of class. This might be especially useful in universities where the students are still adding and dropping classes the first week. If they miss the first day when you hand out and discuss the syllabus, they can still get a copy, read over it, and then participate in the quiz. Figure 2.3 contains a sample syllabus quiz.

A Final Note

Even after going over the syllabus in class, you will always have that one student who claims, "I didn't know the policy on late papers." Consider having the students sign a classroom behavior contract. In this contract they are stating that they have received and understand the syllabus similar to what companies do for employee handbooks. An example of a classroom behavior contract is in Figure 2.4.

One of the things professors tell me is that their syllabi get longer with years of teaching experience. I have to admit this has been true for me. My first class had a syllabus of only one page; I am currently up to ten. I didn't even have written classroom policies until my "Class from Hell" several years ago brought home the importance of setting expectations and enforcing them.

---Dr. Kirk

Figure 2.1: Sample Tips for Success Sheet

Strategies for doing well in this class:
1. Keep up. This sounds obvious, but it's easy to fall behind during a busy week and VERY hard to catch up.
2. Read the appropriate sections of the book <u>before</u> coming to lecture. The syllabus gives specific readings for each lecture. Read with a pencil and paper in hand and work through the sample problems. Having done these two things, you will be prepared to come to the faster paced college-style lecture. If you cannot read the book beforehand, try to pick up what you can from lecture, which will be considerably more difficult to follow, and study from the book outside of class.
3. Don't be afraid to ask questions during lecture if something is unclear or seems different from what you read in the text. Other students probably have the same questions.
4. Go through your notes as soon as possible after each lecture. Do this while the information is fresh in your brain so you'll be more able to recognize where something is missing or unclear in your notes. Using a note-taking format in which you leave space to fill in any extra details later.
5. Do the odd problems in the back of the chapters that have answers first before doing the even exercises without answers. Do the problems before looking at the answers. If you do not know how to begin to answer the problem, then go back to and redo the section in

the text related to the concept. Being able to check your answer to make sure you're doing the problem correctly is helpful but should be checked only after the concepts are understood.

6. Form a study group. Have all members work out problems ahead of time, then get together to discuss any questions the group has. If a member of a study group does not prepare before meeting, don't be afraid to ask him or her to either begin taking more responsibility or find a different group.

7. Take advantage of the professor's office hours.

8. Avoid doing all your studying at one sitting. Cramming may be effective when you need to memorize something, but is a poor technique for learning material (yes, there is a difference). Plan to spend 45-60 minutes each day. Start each study session at a different point in the material. If you start at the beginning each time, you'll know the first part really well and not be able to do any of the last part. Few people can learn from the written word alone. Discussing the concepts and problems with a study group or another individual in the class will help you learn. Writing the information down, making lists of topics, and writing out definitions to new terms are all useful methods. Making and studying with flash cards is helpful in cementing the information.

Source: Ronald Theys,
University of Wisconsin-Fond du Lac

Figure 2.2: Sample FAQ Sheet

Q: How can I stay organized?
Use a three-ring binder with sections for:
1. General Information (syllabus, schedule, etc)
2. Class Notes
3. Activities (done as a part of the lecture)
4. Summaries (usually done at end of a lecture)
5. Labs (done in your groups)
6. Homework
7. Projects (one per unit)
8. Reviews and Tests

Q: What if I miss class?
1. Since we cover so much material in this course, it is never a good idea to miss class. Try not to miss more than 3 classes total.
2. If you miss class, you will not receive credit for labs or quizzes completed that day. I will drop one quiz grade per unit.
3. Contact me if you know you will be absent in order to get the handouts. They will be helpful to you in studying.

Q: I am still not getting it! What can I do?
1. Read the material before class. Are you putting enough time in? Doing the homework?
2. If you need help, see me during office hours.
3. The Math Lab is a wonderful place to get extra help on your homework.
4. Consider forming a study group.

**Source: Paula Thonney,
Brookdale Community College**

Figure 2.3: Sample Quiz on Syllabus

NO   YES   1. Is the final comprehensive?

NO   YES   2. Is attendance taken in this class and used in determining final grades?

NO   YES   3. Will I be expected to participate in class discussion on a regular basis?

NO   YES   4. Will I be graded for participation?

NO   YES   5. Are there team projects in this class?

NO   YES   6. Does the professor have set office hours each week?

NO   YES   7. Is cheating on tests or paper allowed in this class?

NO   YES   8. Am I expected to be in class, seated, and ready to participate at the beginning of class?

NO   YES   9. Will I lose points for excessive tardiness?

_____   10. How many tests, including the final, will there be in this class?

Figure 2.4: Classroom Behavior Contract

1. I have received and read the syllabus for this course.
2. I understand the policy on attendance and tardiness.
3. I understand that I am expected to take exams as noted on the syllabus and to notify my professor before an exam if I have to miss one. Makeup exams are scheduled at the professor's discretion and should be completed within one week of the original date.
4. I understand that the professor expects me to respect her, my classmates, and guest speakers at all times.
5. I understand it is my responsibility to complete and hand in all assignments on time and that there are penalties for late papers.
6. I understand that it is my responsibility to get any handouts that were given out on a day that I missed.
7. I understand that I have two "personal" days during the semester where I can miss class without penalty but that I am expected to let the professor know, either by e-mail or in person, when I plan to take those days.

Signature: _____

Date: _____

Questions from Faculty

Dear Dr. Kirk,
My students seem to want to be entertained in class. Is it our job to make classes interesting and are there some subjects that are just inherently dull?

Not Saying That I Teach Math...

Dear Not a Math Professor,
We have to get our students' attention before they can learn from us. I think any subject can be made more interesting if we try to remember why we got into teaching it in the first place. We need to share that interest with our students. I had a statistics professor when I was in school that taught us probabilities by examining the odds of all the various card games in Las Vegas. Needless to say, we were all glued to the lecture.

Dear Dr. Kirk:
Faculty usually do a good job of telling students what we expect on tests, papers, and other assignments. Do you propose that faculty do the same for expectations on classroom behavior?

B.F. Skinner

Dear B.F.,
Absolutely! I address my expectations for acceptable behavior on my syllabus and in class. Just as I tell them my policy on makeup exams, I tell them what I expect on attendance and classroom behavior.

Comments from Students

Professors need to make their expectations of the students clear and communicate these effectively. Try to use humor; it doesn't even have to be funny.

Jacob

I had a business professor who never cared if students were paying attention, the lecture material was not relevant to the tests, no practice problems were ever gone over, attendance was not mandatory, and class was strictly lecture. I hated the class.

Dana

My bad professors did not have rules with students as far as coming in late, talking in class, leaving early, etc. Also, I have had conceited professors who have an "aura" that they are better than the student. One of my professors didn't even bother to update old tests even though we hadn't covered all the material in class.

Michael

The best professor I ever had definitely knew how to teach students because I have retained most of the information. A combination of lectures, class discussion/interaction, team presentations, and exams testing the material taught seemed to be the right formula. It was an interesting and fun class.

Justin

Endnote:
[1]Huba, Mary E. and Jann E. Freed, *Learner-Centered Assessment on College Campuses: Shifting the Focus From Teaching to Learning*, Allyn and Bacon, 2000.

CHAPTER 3

Managing the First Impression

*I've learned that nervous
speakers make people nervous.*
                    ---Rev. Jesse Jackson

Speaking in public is the thing that most people dread more than death. Compound this with the desire to get off to a good start (as you will be walking into that classroom for the next four months or so) and you can understand the anxiety many teachers face. There is a lot of pressure to make a good first impression.

> *Every new semester as I walk into my classroom, I am a little nervous...even after 25 years of teaching experience. And it's ok. I think when I get to the point where I don't feel this anxiety, I won't be as effective a teacher.*
> **---Dr. Kirk**

Importance of First Impressions
Research shows that people make assumptions about our credibility, professionalism, and sincerity within a few seconds of meeting us for the first time. The "way we package and present ourselves as a whole—including personal appearance, body language, voice quality, attitude, and behavior—plays a large part in how others judge us..."[1]

This emphasis on first impressions translates to the classroom as well. Frank Bernieri of Oregon State University conducted an experiment where he discussed his syllabus the first day of class and then had the students filled out a teaching evaluation form. At the end of the semester, they completed the same form. He found the rating the students gave him at the end of the semester was essentially the same as that given the first day. According to Bernieri, if your students think the class will be interesting and useful and that you are a credible professor on the first day, they will tend to think that throughout the semester. In fact, Bernieri states that people will make excuses and manipulate the data in order to reinforce their first impressions.[2]

Nalini Ambady of Tufts University concurs with Bernieri. She conducted a study where she showed students a ten second video of professors they had never met. Their ratings of the professors in the videos were the same as those given by students who had the professors in class for several months.[3] In addition, the students' first impression of whether the professor was an effective teacher predicted how well the students themselves performed on tests. According to Ambady, "students learned more from teachers who were seen...as having the qualities of a better teacher."[4]

Preparing for the first day of class by deciding what to wear, how you want to be addressed, and working on your presentation skills will help you make a good first impression.

Before Class Begins

Preparation for how you will conduct the first day really begins before the semester or quarter starts. Check out the classroom layout, determine where you will stand, and make sure you know how to work the equipment in the room. Doing this will help you reduce your anxiety on the first day of class and thus create a good first impression. Be sure to avoid fussing with your papers, the projector, or computer equipment when you get there. You should already have the equipment ready to go and your notes organized so that you appear confident.

What to Wear

James Lang of Assumption College writes of his experience in a summer class when he walked in wearing shorts, golf shirt, and sandals. An adult student in the class asked him if he was the professor. When he replied affirmatively, she commented, "You don't look like a professor."[5]

Consider how you will dress for class. How you dress reflects your own sense of self-worth and shows your students that you respect them enough to dress professionally. You might want to dress conservatively if you are young, a female, or a minority in order to be taken more seriously by your students. Your dress sends a message to the students as to how you view yourself and the class, and will help you establish credibility. Students should not err in thinking that you are just another student when you walk in. Thus, your clothing and demeanor should project leadership. Consider dressing the way you would if you were meeting with other experts in your field. Most students expect their professors to dress more formally than the students do.

Choose How You Want to be Addressed

You will need to give some thought as to how you will introduce yourself. Will you allow your students to address you by your first name or will you introduce yourself as Professor or Dr.? Using a title, even if it is Mr. or Mrs., will establish that you are in charge. It is easier to be a little more formal and strict at the beginning of the semester and then loosen up than it is to be casual at first and then decide to be strict. Many times professors err in wanting to be "liked" by their students. Remember, you are in the classroom to teach students, not to be their best friend.

Show Confidence

Your students are making judgments about you during the first few minutes of class. Everything, including how you dress, walk, and present yourself, is being evaluated. Additionally, the culture of the classroom is being established which will affect how the students behave in the classroom and thus how effective you will be as the teacher.

Walk briskly and with purpose into the classroom. Chat with your students as they come into the room to make yourself, and the students, feel comfortable. It is important to present yourself as confident about what you will be doing the first day.

Do not tell your students that you are nervous as this makes the students uncomfortable and you will lose credibility with them. Also, never tell your students that this is the first time you have taught this particular course. You know more about the topic than they do or your university would not have hired you. Let the students assume you are an expert.

As you begin the class, make eye contact with two or three people in various parts of the room. You are essentially beginning to build a relationship with your students. Be enthusiastic about being in the classroom so that the students will be as well. Don't just stand behind the podium but move around and toward them. Look happy to be sharing your knowledge with them.

Your presentation skills
Work on your presentation skills by videotaping your lecture or having a colleague sit in on a class to discover any nervous habits you might have. Students are easily distracted by gestures and body language. Also, be aware of the overuse of hesitation sounds such as "ah" and "uhm" or filler words such as "you know" and "like." These make you sound unsure of yourself. According to Laurie Haleta at South Dakota State University, our use of filler words, tag questions, and disclaimers affect the students' perception of our credibility, control of the classroom, and command of our subject matter.[6]

> *I had a lecture hall teacher that said 'ah' so many times that the students started paying very close attention...to his 'ah's!" They were actually counting them and making bets on how often he would say it.*
> **---Aaron, 2003 graduate**
> **Iowa State University**

You might also take a course from Toastmasters. Toastmasters has over 10,000 clubs with 200,000 members and is an organization that helps people improve their presentation skills, learn how to give constructive evaluations, and become better listeners.[7]

A Final Note

Give a lot of thought as to what first impressions you are giving your students. This will help you to establish your credibility and gain control of your classroom. Chapter 4 discusses how to use that first impression on the first day of class.

> *When I first began teaching, I was giving a lecture to a class where I would unconsciously bang on the podium whenever I made an important point. Thank goodness after a couple of weeks of doing this, a student in the front of the room banged back on his desk, making me aware of what I was doing and I stopped.*
> **---Dr. Kirk**

Questions from Faculty

Dear Dr. Kirk:
Can you give me some tips to deal with nervousness? Even after five years of teaching, I still find myself anxious upon entering the classroom.

Nervous Nelly

Dear Nelly,
First of all, never tell your students that you are nervous as this will affect your credibility. Try developing a routine to help with the nervousness. Take a short brisk walk before class to loosen up your body and prevent your knees from shaking. Twirl your wrists and gently shake the stress out of your arms. This helps to increase your circulation which in turn will reduce anxiety. Be sure and relax your shoulders; people tend to "hunch up" their shoulders when tense. Do some deep breathing. Above all, talk positively to yourself: "I've got this lecture down cold. I can't wait to get in there and help these students learn."

Dear Dr. Kirk:
What is with college students today? They are demanding, extremely vocal, think they know it all, and don't want to do the work I assign. I have been teaching 15 years and am at a loss as to what is happening and how to handle this generation of college students. Any suggestions?

At a Loss at Midwestern College

Dear At a Loss,

Yes, they are demanding, vocal, and think they know it all. They are also smart, technologically competent, multi-taskers who want to know why the work you are assigning is going to be useful for them to do. Don't get me wrong. I don't think our students are bad. I think there is a great deal of pressure on them today. All of my students have double majors, jobs or internships of 30+ hours a week, are active in organizations, have team projects in most of their classes, etc. They believe that they have to do all of these things in order to get a good job. They have little patience for "busy work." Our job is to show them how the course work is useful to understanding the topics being taught.

Comments from Students

I really appreciate a professor who takes the time to learn my name.

Caiti

My worse professor taught statistics. He answered his cell phone in class, showed up late often, forgot to make copies of quizzes, and spoke about one chapter for over a week, long after we had all gotten it.

Belma

I have had a lot of intelligent professors in college; however, some of them did not know how to communicate the material to the students or make the class interesting.

Irina

I had a biology professor who spoke in a very monotone voice with no passion or enthusiasm in his lecture.

Andrea

The worst professor I've had taught management courses. She is really ineffective because she talks down to the class, not condescendingly, but acts like we're 3 years old and can't figure anything out for ourselves. She is excessively redundant and spends 20 minutes explaining how she's going to explain something. She's really nice, just ineffective.

Kelly

Endnotes:
[1]Everett, Lesley, "Dress to Impress," *Personnel Today*, November 18, 2003, p. 24.
[2]Bernieri, Frank, "OSU Prof's Summer Class to Cast New Light on First Impressions," http://oregonstate.edu/dept/ncs/newsarch/2004/Jun04/impressions.htm
[3]Ambady, Nalini, and R. Rosenthal, "Half a Minute: Predicting Teacher Evaluations from Thin Slices of Behavior and Physical Attractiveness, *Journal of Personality and Social Psychology*, 1993, vol 64(3), pp. 431-441.
[4]Winerman, Lea, "'Thin Slices' of Life," http://www.apa.org/monitor/mar05/slices/html
[5]Lang, James M., "Looking Like a Professor," *Chronicle of Higher Education*, July 27, 2005.
[6]Haleta, Laurie L, "Student Perceptions of Teachers' Use of Language: The Effects of Powerful and Powerless Language on Impression Formation and Uncertainty," *Communication Education*, January 1996, vol 45, pp. 16-28.
[7]See www.toastmasters.com

CHAPTER 4

Managing the First Day of Class

The more you prepare outside class, the less you perspire in class. The less you perspire in class, the more you inspire the class.

Ho Boon Tiong

The first day of class is exciting and scary for both the student and the professor. Most students decide the first day how they feel about the course, the subject matter, other students in the class, and the teacher.

Some professors spend very little time in the classroom on the first day and just hand out the syllabus. This may reduce the professor's anxiety but it also tells the students that the class time is not really important. Others use the time to deliver a full lecture on the first chapter of the textbook which tends to overwhelm the students. A middle ground is probably more appropriate.

Certainly the syllabus should be discussed as there is little guarantee the students will read it on their own (how many of us have really read our faculty handbook from cover to cover?). Keep in mind that the students probably have several classes and will not be able to remember everything said about the syllabus. Therefore, it will be important to go over various deadlines and expectations about future assignments again as the semester progresses.

Establish Your Credibility

It is important to give a brief outline of your academic credentials, work background, and teaching experiences. Illustrate to your students why you are qualified to teach this class. Tell a "war story" from your work experiences to show that you have made mistakes as well. Explain why you went into teaching. Show your enthusiasm about the course content and why you think this particular class is important to the students.

Set Expectations the First Day

It is important to set your expectations of the class on the first day. If one of your classroom policies is coming to class on time, make sure that you are also on time or even a few minutes early. If you have a cell phone, bring it with you and make a display of turning it off before class. To emphasize that you are taking the class seriously, give the students an assignment to do that will be collected at the next class meeting. Another alternative is to assign some reading to do and announce that you will have a short quiz on the material during the second class. If the class involves writing, then have them write. If you will be using cases, then do a short case. Keep in mind that on the first day of class, students are trying to figure out what your expectations will be.

Involve the Students

Have students fill out an info sheet or index card with their name, major, phone number, e-mail address, etc. Ask for additional information such as their knowledge of the course content and whether they have taken any related classes on the subject matter. If you are teaching a quantitative course, you might ask how comfortable the students are with math. In an English composition class, you might inquire about their past writing experience.

I use the following question on my info sheet when teaching a quantitative course so that I can get a sense of which students will need extra help.

<u>*How comfortable are you with math?*</u>
____ *Math is my middle name.*
____ *I can do math problems if I have to.*
____ *I recognize numbers when I see them.*
____ *They had to drag me kicking and*
     screaming into this math course.

---Dr. Kirk

Another good question to ask students is what they hope to get out of the class. Be prepared for answers such as "a good grade" or "it's a requirement for my major." You might want to emphasize that it is assumed that everyone wants to do well in the class and you are looking for some more specific answers.

Ask your students if they have a job or internship and what they do in the organization in which they work. After a few weeks of class when you have started learning your students' names, go back and read over the info cards. The information will be more meaningful to you at this point and you can use it at appropriate moments in the class. For example, say, "Susan, can you tell us how your company conducts its exit interviews?"

> *One semester I had a student that worked for UPS while they were going through union contract negotiations. He was able to provide great examples for my Labor Relations course.*
> **---Dr. Kirk**

Another benefit to using info cards is that it takes the students' attention away from you and toward filling out the cards. This provides you a few minutes to get comfortable with this new class of students. The cards also communicate that you are interested in them as individuals which contributes to a positive first impression.

Discuss the Syllabus
Pass out the syllabus and go over the important points. Do not read directly from the syllabus. Students assume that if you read the syllabus to them, you will read from the book the rest of the semester, which is something they hate. Instead give more detail and ask for questions. Explain what the class is about and how it fits in with other courses in the college. Consider putting sample test questions and answers on the syllabus and discuss a couple of these during the class.

Introduce the Textbook

Introduce the textbook by using a copy as a visual aid. Explain how you want them to use the book. Will they be expected to read the chapters before you lecture on that subject or afterwards? Is the book the main source of information or a supplement to the lectures? Do not criticize the book's author or the book itself as the students will wonder why they had to purchase it. Explain any discrepancies and why you have your particular viewpoint if it is different from that of the book author. Also, explain how you will test if there is a discrepancy.

Conduct an Icebreaker

Consider an icebreaker the first day of class so that you can start getting to know your students. Depending on the class size, a good icebreaker is to have the students introduce themselves to you. Go around the room and ask each student for their name, major, and one unusual thing about them that will help you to remember them. Not only does this help you and the students learn each others' names, it sets the tone that the students are expected to actively participate in the class.

> *I still remember the student who told me she had written John Travolta and asked him to her senior prom (he didn't attend but did send an autographed photo). Another student revealed that everyone in her family had red hair including the cat.*
>
> **---Dr. Kirk**

Another icebreaker is to have students stand up and find a partner. The two students are to throw out things to each other that they might have in common such as "oldest child," "from Chicago," or "majoring in journalism." When they find something, they both raise their hands and give a "high five." After they find three things in common, they do a little "happy dance" and sit down. As you can imagine, this provides a great deal of energy and enthusiasm in the classroom.

If your class is large, you can still involve the students by asking questions that require them to raise their hands. You might ask for specific majors; whether they are freshmen, sophomores, juniors or seniors; how many are graduating that semester; how many are working, etc. You could also put them into small groups of four to five students and ask them to discuss with their group what they have heard about the class or about you as the professor. This gives you a chance to correct misconceptions or reinforce them. Figure 4.1 gives some examples of icebreakers used by other colleagues.

Establish the Class Culture
Remember that on the first day, students are trying to figure out the class culture. This includes whether the classroom will be formal or informal, whether the professor has a sense of humor, how much student discussion will be expected, etc. Give the students an idea of what they, and you, will be doing in the class.

First Day Exercise

Instead of lecturing the first day or letting the students go early, consider putting together an exercise that will illustrate what you will be doing throughout the semester. The goal is to get the students excited and participating in the class subject matter right away. Figure 4.2 is an example of an exercise developed for use in a human resource management class.

For a first day exercise, I put the students into teams and ask them to consider the issues involved in a real-life scenario. I don't expect the students to know what laws or concepts apply. I just want them to start thinking about the class subject matter. I am also illustrating that we will be doing cases in class, that they will work in teams to address these cases, and that I expect everyone to participate. I am attempting to create a class culture so that the students will get to know their classmates and me and feel comfortable voicing their opinions. I do this by walking around the room and participating in the various group discussions, throwing out other issues or questions for them to consider. I know I have had a good first day of class when the students are reluctant to leave and are still discussing the case in the hallway with each other or with me afterwards.

---Dr. Kirk

Another example of a good first day exercise is in Marielle Hoefnagels' article, *"Using Superstitions and Sayings to Teach Experimental De-*

sign."[1] Groups of students are assigned various superstitions such as, "An apple a day keeps the doctor away" or "Breaking a mirror will result in seven years of bad luck." The students then have to develop ways to test these "hypotheses." She uses this assignment in her biology classes but it would work equally well for a number of other courses including research methods, statistics, insurance, and marketing.

Student Feedback

Consider asking the students to write down any questions they still have at the end of the class. Tell them not to put their names on the papers and that they can ask you anything. This provides you feedback on what the students were afraid to ask in class. It also establishes that they are responsible for their own learning if there is something they do not understand.

A Final Note

Figure 4.3 contains a quick checklist to help you organize the first day of class. Use it to manage the first impressions you want the students to have of you as someone who is credible, organized, and competent.

> *Don't be afraid to have high expectations for student conduct in the classroom. You are not asking your students to do anything that you would not expect of yourself: go to class on time, refrain from leaving in the middle of class, and turn off your cell phone.*
> **---Dr. Kirk**

Figure 4.1: Icebreaker Suggestions

For my international courses I generally ask a series of questions such as how many countries the students have been to, languages they speak, and their most exciting or unusual international stories. If they are a little shy, I start sharing some of my own travel stories, and that usually relaxes them.

---Vinitia Mathews, University of Iowa

I have a bag of trinkets I have collected that includes a pencil, spoon, gum, whiteout, string, lots of McDonald's kids toys, etc. If I am teaching a smaller class, less than 40, I have them pick something from the bag that represents their personality. They have to share that item along with their personal introduction. In my large Principles of Management class (400 students) I have them break into groups of 4-5. They introduce themselves, where they are from, their major, and phone numbers so that everyone knows at least one person in the class. Then they have to identify the five most important things that a manager does. After they have done that, I have someone serve as scribe. Then I go through the class with my wireless microphone and get a representative of most of the teams to share what they thought. When we are done, we basically have an outline of the class. I'm able to say, "Good, these are the things we are going to talk about during the course this semester." It offers a nice intro to the class.

---Charlotte D. Sutton, Auburn University

Figure 4.1 (con't)

One of my students told me a trick used in the business he works for that I would like to try. He said they pass around a roll of toilet paper and tell everyone to pull off as many pieces as they would need for a one night camping trip. Then everyone has to tell one thing about themselves for each sheet of paper they have...of course they do not know that at first. Even if they take a lot of paper they can say little things like my hair is really blonde, etc. He claims it works very well.

---Dee Sams, University of South Florida

One technique the students like is BINGO! I put different descriptors in each block and they have to go around and talk to people to see if they fit in their block. For example, one block says "Find someone who can name all seven dwarfs" or "Find someone who has bungee jumped." They need to talk a little with that person because if they get BINGO first, they have to introduce the people they used in the BINGO line. They have fun and I usually put one on that I'm sure I'm the only one who can answer, like "Find someone who knows how to do regression analysis." Eventually they come up and say, Dr. Leonard, can we use you?

---Nancy H. Leonard,
West Virginia University

Figure 4.2: Example of
1st Day Class Exercise

<u>Can employees be fired for off-duty behavior?</u>
Peter Oiler, a truck driver for Winn-Dixie Stores, was always on time with excellent performance appraisals. While at work, he followed the company's dress code. However, the 47-year-old liked to cross dress, wearing women's clothing, makeup, and wigs in his personal life. He would go out with his wife and friends as "Donna" to restaurants, stores, and to church. When Winn-Dixie learned of his off-the-job behavior, they fired him. Oiler then sued for sex discrimination, claiming that Winn-Dixie fired him because he did not fit the stereotype of a man.

1. What are the issues involved here? Can a company fire an employee for off-duty behavior such as cross dressing?
2. Can a company fire an employee for other off-duty behaviors such as the following?
   - Employee drinking alcohol on the weekend?
   - Employee getting drunk while wearing company logo on his shirt?
   - Accountant arrested for embezzling church donations?
   - Accountant convicted of domestic abuse?
   - Employee sentenced to six months jail time for drunk driving?

Based on case: Peter Oiler v. Winn-Dixie Louisiana, Inc. Civil Action No. 00-3114 (Sect. I).

Figure 4.3: Checklist for the First Day

1. Did I write on the board as well as announce orally how I want to be addressed in this class?

2. Was I enthusiastic about the class and subject matter?

3. Did I go over my syllabus and discuss my expectations?

4. Have I established my credibility?

5. Did I use an ice-breaker to involve the students?

6. Did I gather information on the students' backgrounds and start learning their names?

7. Did I keep the students the entire class period to establish that I believe the class to be important?

8. Did I present some background of the subject matter to give the students some sense of what the course is about?

9. Did I explain how this class fits in with other courses in the college?

10. Have I established the culture or tone of the class?

Questions from Faculty

Dear Dr. Kirk:
How do you distinguish between a student who is respectful but disagrees with what you are saying and one who means to challenge your authority?

Unsure About His Intentions

Dear Unsure,
I had a male student that disagreed with me every day of class when I first began my teaching career. After several weeks of this, I realized it was becoming disruptive to the class as well as upsetting me. I met with him after class, said I thought we had a personality conflict, and offered to sign his drop slip. He backed down, said there wasn't a problem, and behaved from then on. Sometimes I think you can tell from the students' tone and body language whether they are truly interested in learning and whether they are challenging your authority. Letting them know that you know what they are doing helps.

Dear Professor Kirk:
I have one student who reads the newspaper each day during my lecture. What should I do?

---Should I Even Care?

Dear Should You Care,
Yes. The rest of the class is aware of what the student is doing and watching to see how you will handle this. Soon you will have two students reading the newspaper. If you don't say anything, you have essentially said it is ok for

the student to continue. Talk to the student and explain your expectations for classroom behavior.

Comments from Students

My worse professor taught computer science and he was the most boring guy I have ever taken a class from. By the end of the semester he was lucky to still have 10 out of the 30 students who originally enrolled in class. He did not explain the material, just assumed we all were computer programmers, and then lost everyone's interest when he told lame stories not relevant to class.

Greg

I had an adjunct professor for finance who obviously wasn't a people person. He was very talented in the subject but didn't know how to teach it, nothing applied to real life, and he went so fast people couldn't follow.

Nick

Another bad teacher was one who taught night class in economics. This person on the first day told us that he worked for the state and was teaching for extra income. He went on to say that it is not his job to teach economics but to be an administrator or proctor for the class. It was our job to learn everything before we came to class and we would then be quizzed on it. He made us feel we were not important and were wasting his time.

Carl

My professor would actually get mad when people didn't understand and had to ask questions as he would think of it as holding the class behind.

Sarah

Endnote:

[1]Hoefnagels, Marielle, *"Using Superstitions and Sayings to Teach Experimental Design,"* found at http://www.zoo.utoronto.ca/able/volumes/vol-24/mini.16.hoefnagels.pdf

CHAPTER 5

Managing Sexual Harassment
in the Classroom

*Universities should be safe havens where
ruthless examination of realties will not
be distorted by the aim to please or
inhibited by the risk of displeasure.*
---Kingman Brewster
President, Yale University, 1964

As many as 20 to 50 percent of female students
have been or will be sexually harassed during
their college years.[1] The number of complaints
and lawsuits has skyrocketed in academia as
well as in the business world. Universities are
realizing that they need to address the issue of
dating between faculty and students. Duke University and Ohio Wesleyan have recently written
policies addressing consensual sexual relationships between students and faculty. Universities such as the College of William and Mary and
the University of Iowa forbid such relationships
if the professor employs or a3dvises the student.
Stanford University cautions their professors
that getting involved with a student might not be
a wise career decision.[2]

Part of the job of a professor is to conduct a class
that is free of harassment so that students can

feel safe in the learning environment. This chapter presents legal and professional obligations that faculty have for protecting students from sexual harassment. In addition, suggestions are made to help faculty be proactive in protecting themselves from sexual harassment claims.

What is Sexual Harassment?

Sexual harassment claims vary from blatant misuse of power by faculty to relationships gone awry. Some instances may just be cases of eager faculty wanting to be liked by their students. The following list illustrates the gamut of actual sexual harassment claims in universities and thus the difficulty of defining just what is sexual harassment.

- A political science professor at State University of New York was sued by a female student because he called her "Monica" and pointed out that she resembled Monica Lewinsky. He allegedly made numerous comments about Clinton and cigars.[3]

- An English professor at Macomb Community College was suspended for using lewd language in class. The court ruled that his rights to academic freedom did not allow him to compromise his students' rights to a classroom environment free of vulgar language that was not germane to the topics being discussed.[4]

- At Ohio Wesleyan University, Professor Conrad Kent had a consensual relationship with a 23-year-old female student while she was at the college. The affair ended when she returned to her home country. A year later, she was arrested for stalking Professor Kent via the Internet. When the relationship became public, he was disciplined even though he claimed the university had known about the affair.[5]

- A tenured professor at the University of Tennessee was fired for inviting students to his house after being warned not to do this because of the potential for "compromising professional relationships between faculty and students."[6]

- At Cornell University, a professor was found guilty of sexually harassing four female students. The faculty committee that investigated the case recommended that he be fired if he harassed students again. In addition, the committee suggested that an award for "distinguished teaching" be taken away from him. The professor, however, stated he had not meant his comments to be sexual or romantic. Rather, he had wanted the students to feel like part of the "Cornell family." In fact, the teaching award honored the professor for creating an atmosphere of intimacy in his classes.[7]

As you can see, some of these claims are obviously inappropriate while others may be cases of poor judgment.

Sexual harassment is a type of sex discrimination actionable under the Civil Rights Act of 1964. Title VII of the Act covers sex discrimination where the student is an employee at a university such as in a work/study program. Title IX prohibits sex discrimination in the classroom and other activities and organizations within the university.[8]

According to the Supreme Court, there are two types of sexual harassment: *quid pro quo* and *hostile environment. Quid pro quo* (a Latin phrase that translates as, "something for something") involves some type of exchange, such as sexual favors in return for a internship or good grades. Since this type of sexual harassment involves a power relationship where the professor or work supervisor has authority over the student, the university is automatically liable for the actions of its faculty or staff. *Hostile environment* is defined as an intimidating, offensive, or "hostile" environment. Professors, staff, administrators, other students, or even persons outside the university such as vendors or guest speakers can create this offensive environment. In this type of sexual harassment, the hostile environment would have to be severe or pervasive enough as to interfere with the student's employment or education. The university would be liable if it knew about the harassment and did not take timely steps to correct the situation.[9]

Quid pro quo harassment is easier to recognize than *hostile environment.* Defining hostile environment is more challenging as what is offensive to one person might not be to another; it tends to be a matter of perception. Thus, it is difficult to develop an all-encompassing list of inappropriate behaviors. It is important that each complaint be examined on a case-by-case basis by looking at the nature of the sexual harassment and the context in which the alleged incidents occurred.

The following list provides guidance on both types of sexual harassment.

- Both men and women can be victims of sexual harassment, and both women and men can be guilty of harassing others. Thus, a female professor can harass a male student.

- The harasser does not have to be the victim's professor. He or she may be a supervisor, staff member, fellow student, or guest to the university. For example, a soft drink vendor could be guilty of sexually harassing students in their dorms.

- The victim does not have to be of the opposite sex from the harasser. The crucial issue is whether the harasser treats a member or members of one sex differently from members of the other sex, as sexual harassment is a form of sex discrimination. An illustration is a male professor making lewd comments to his male students but not to his female ones.

- The victim does not have to be the person at whom the unwelcome sexual conduct is directed. He or she may be someone who is affected by such conduct when it is directed towards another person. For example, lewd comments or dirty jokes told by one male student to another male but overheard by a female student may be offensive to the female and constitute a hostile environment.

- There is no requirement that the victim complains to the harasser or reports the sexual harassment. In fact, a student may be afraid to say anything for fear of losing his or her job or getting a poor grade. The university can still be held liable for sexual harassment if the behavior is so blatant that an administrator should have known that the harassment occurred but failed to take appropriate corrective action.

- A finding of sexual harassment does not depend on the victim having suffered a concrete economic injury. Thus, a student could file a sexual harassment charge even though he or she does not receive negative working conditions or poor grades. A case of this might be male students complaining that their professor favors the female students in class, giving them higher grades and consideration.

Counseling Students

There are several steps you can advise students to take if they believe they have been sexually harassed. These can range from seeking informal advice from you or another professor to making a formal complaint with the university. A final resort would be filing a lawsuit. Obviously, the university would prefer that the situation be resolved successfully within the organization.

If a student shares a harassment incident with you confidentially, you are not legally obligated to inform the administration of your university. However, the university may have a policy requiring you to report the incident to the human resources manager or another designated person without naming the parties involved. Doing this will allow the designated office to spot any major problems or trends and still respect the confidence of the student.

Many times when students come to you with a sexual harassment incident, they want advice on how to handle the situation. Suggest that they tell the person harassing them that they are uncomfortable with the behavior and ask the harasser to stop. Tell the student that if the harassment does not stop, the student may need to follow more formal complaint procedures. Be sure to follow up afterwards and ask the student if the situation has improved. Document any sensitive information that a student might share with you. Include what was said, the date and time, what advice you gave, and what actions you took.

If you are a department chair, dean, or other university administrator, you are legally required to follow-up on any sexual harassment claims that are brought to your attention. You should advise the student that anything shared will be investigated. Also, state that it will be necessary for the student's identity to be revealed, but that will only be done on a "need to know" basis. Thus, only those involved in the harassment situation, potential witnesses, and those investigating the case will need to know the student's identity.

Advice for Faculty

Research indicates that there is a fine line between the perception of friendliness by a professor and the perception of sexual harassment by the student.[10] Some tips for faculty to avoid being misunderstood by students are:

- Be aware of how students perceive you. Do not have a reputation as someone who makes inappropriate comments or acts unprofessionally.
- In class, do not focus on one gender to the exclusion of the other gender. Do not show favoritism in any way.
- Do not refer to an adult as doll, babe, or honey.
- When students come to your office, leave the door open.
- If a student appears to be romantically interested in you, avoid being or speaking with them alone. If necessary to meet, choose a public place such as your university cafeteria. Consider asking another

faculty member to join you.
- Never date or express interest in dating a student who is in one of your classes.
- Do not ask personal questions about a student's social or sexual life.
- Avoid lewd or vulgar language in your classes.
- Do not use sexual innuendoes or tell dirty jokes to your students.
- Do not use sexually suggestive visuals in class.
- Avoid making comments about a student's hair or clothing.
- Be sure that your grading process is documented and based on objective criteria.
- Look at the sexual harassment policy that your university has adopted and consider including it on your syllabus.

A Final Note

It should be noted that not all sexual harassment charges are true. In the *Journal of Management Education*, Timothy Serey wrote about his experience with a false harassment accusation.[11] He discusses the feelings of anguish and anger he experienced in dealing with a situation he never thought could happen to him. That article emphasizes that faculty need to be professional and above reproach at all time. You should also be aware of your responsibilities in situations that might be considered sexual harassment.

Be mindful that your university's legal counsel is there to protect the university, not individual faculty members. If you are accused of harassment by a student, consider hiring your own attorney.

> *I have a friend who was recently accused of sexual harassment at his university. He claims he is innocent; however, some of his colleagues find this difficult to believe as he has a reputation earned over many years for dating his students.*
>
> **---Dr. Kirk**

Questions from Faculty

Dear Dr. Kirk:
One of my advisees, Sara, has come to me and complained about sexual comments made by a teaching assistant, John, concerning her appearance. Some of these comments about her clothing and body were made in front of other students, which she says made her feel uncomfortable. Sara states that she and John have a good relationship and thus she does not want him to know that she has come to me about this matter. Sara wants John's behavior to stop. What should I do?

Faculty Advisor

Dear Faculty Advisor,
Because the comments made by John are of a sexual nature and they make Sara uncomfortable, this would constitute hostile environment sexual harassment and thus is actionable under Title VII of the Civil Rights Act. Sara has asked you not to confront John and as her advisor, it is important that you respect her wishes. As you are not in a position of authority for the university (as department chairperson or dean), you are not obligated to report the harassment. However, if one student has been made uncomfortable enough to come to you, it is very possible that others feel the same way about John. The best way to handle this would be to go to your department chair and/or dean and tell him or her what has happened without identifying anyone involved. The administrator should then send out a memo to all teaching assistants stating the

university's policy on sexual harassment, along with a definition and examples of what constitutes sexual harassment, and possible consequences of not complying with the policy. You should then follow up with Sara at a later date to see if the behavior has stopped. If not, then a more direct method may be necessary. Another approach might be for your College to require all teaching assistants to attend a sexual harassment workshop.

Dear Dr. Kirk:
I have a male student, Bill, whom I have overheard tell "dirty" jokes in the classroom before class actually begins. Both the male and female students laugh when Bill tells these jokes so I didn't think much of it. However, I have assigned Bill to a team with Mary and she has now come to me and complained about Bill's jokes. Is this sexual harassment? What should I do?

Jack, Management Professor

Dear Jack,
Yes, this is sexual harassment. Bill is creating a hostile environment for Mary. This is an excellent opportunity for you to create a "teaching moment" that will help Bill and others learn about appropriate behavior in the workplace. As the professor you should introduce the topic of sexual harassment in your class and give a number of examples of potential harassment including the telling of dirty jokes. In addition, if you should overhear any more inappropriate comments, you should address these on the spot. Mary should also be told to let Bill know that she

is uncomfortable with the jokes if he should continue with this behavior in their team setting.

Dear Dr. Kirk:
Here's an unusual one for you. A student of mine, Amy, recently told me that another student in my class, Bob, has been making inappropriate comments as well as touching her and other female students. The situation is complicated by the fact that Amy has been hired to take notes in class for Bob as he is legally blind. Most of the comments and touching allegedly take place at Bob's apartment when they are supposed to be studying for class. Amy does not want to hurt Bob's feelings but is uncomfortable with the situation and is considering giving up the scribe job. She does not want me to say anything to Bob but she wants his behavior to stop. What should I do?
Professor Trying to be Politically Correct

Dear Professor Trying,
This is an unusual case dealing with student-to-student sexual harassment with an added twist that the harasser has a disability. As both Amy and Bob are students in your class, you are obligated to resolve this situation. An indirect way might be to open up a discussion on sexual harassment in class, asking students to role-play the different forms that hostile environment sexual harassment can take. However, since other students that are not in the class are involved, a more direct approach may be necessary. One suggestion would be to require that all future study sessions take place at the university in-

stead of Bob's home. If you are not comfortable approaching Bob about this, I would suggest that you convince Amy to file an informal complaint with your university's human resources director. The director will then be able to interview the other female students involved and then discuss the situation with Bob. It is very likely that Bob's behavior is unintentional and that he does not realize that he is making the female students uncomfortable. This way he does not have to be embarrassed that you, as his professor, are aware of the issue. Follow up with Amy to make sure there are no further problems.

Dear Dr. Kirk:
One of my faculty members, Sam, is dating a student of his, Sally. Several students have come to me as Sam's department chair to complain about favoritism shown by Sam to Sally in the classroom as well as on quizzes and tests. Today Sally told me that she and Sam are no longer dating and that she is concerned that this will affect her grade. What do I tell Sally? What do I tell the other students? What actions do I take with Sam? Could the university be liable here?
Worried Department Chair

Dear Worried Chair,
This is a difficult situation dealing with both traditional and third-party harassment. Check your university's policy on faculty dating students. Many universities have written policies prohibiting sexual relationships, even if consensual, between faculty and students they supervise, evaluate, or advise.

Both Sally and the other students should be re-assured that Sam is a professional and will not penalize anyone's grade. You should also give the students a copy of the university's grievance policy and inform them that if they believe they have been discriminated against or treated un-fairly, they have the right to file a complaint.

As a department chairperson, you must follow up on the students' grievances. A written record should be made of the complaints. Sam should be counseled as to the university's policy and cautioned not to retaliate against the students. Follow-up should be made to ensure there are no further problems.

Comments from Students

I had a professor who was disrespectful to students. The professor used to make fun of students during class because he thought it was funny and some of the other students thought it was funny. The professor had favorites in the class and let everyone else know about it and it also showed in the grades that were distributed.

Andrew

I had a bad professor who had a "God" complex; at the start of class he told us that none of us were "A" students, at best we were "B" students, which is slightly above average and most of us were simply average so we got a "C" and just the stupid students got below a "C". This class was amazingly enough a psychology class...this professor also hadn't changed his lesson plans in 10 years although the book had changed a number of times.

Tiffany

My worst professor was an English teacher who was very flamboyant and dressed improperly. The class seemed to have hardly anything to do with English. Plus he loved to brag about his dissertation.

Aaron B.

Endnotes:

[1]Dzeich, B.W. and L. Weiner, *The Lecherous Professor: Sexual Harassment* on Campus, Boston: Beacon Press, 1990; Dreifus, C. "The Dirty Little Secret of Campus Life," *Glamour,* 1986.

[2]Bartlett, Thomas, "The Question of Sex Between Professors and Students," *Chronicle of Higher Education,* April 5, 2002.

[3]Loomis, Tamara, "Harassment Suit Against Professor Can Go Forward," *New York Law Journal,* December, 2003.

[4]Bonnell v. Lorenzo (Macomb Community College), 241 F.3d 800 (6th Cir. 2001).

5Same as 2.

[6]"Did Tennessee Professor Break Sexual Harassment Rules?" *HR On Campus,* October 3, 2002.

[7]Wilson, R. "Harassment charges at Cornell U.," *The Chronicle of Higher Education,* February 10, 1995.

[8]Meritor Savings Bank, FSB v. Vinson et al, 106 S.Ct. 2399 (1986).

[9]Euben, Donna, *Sexual Harassment in the Academy: Some Suggestions for Faculty Policies and Procedures,* October 2002, found at www.aaup. org

[10]Mongeau, P. A. & Blalock, J., "Student Evaluations of Instructor Immediacy and Sexually Harassing Behaviors: An Experimental Investigation," *Journal of Applied Communication Research,* 1994.

[11]Serey, Timothy, "When Lightning Strikes: Dealing With a False Harassment Accusation," *Journal of Management Education,* 1995.

CHAPTER 6

Managing Diversity in the Classroom

*Education's purpose is to replace an
empty mind with an open one.*
---Malcolm S. Forbes

Universities have a much more diverse student population today than in the past. College students range in ages from the traditional 18-year-old right out of high school to those in their 30s, 40s, and 50s coming back to retool. There is an increase in the number of women, students of different races, and students from different countries in the classroom. More and more students have physical or learning disabilities. They come in with a wide range of abilities, skills, and motivations. Managing such a diverse student population is challenging even to professors who have been teaching for many years.

It is important to respect each of your students as individuals and refrain from comments and behaviors that might make them feel excluded from the class. The following list presents suggestions to help you make a connection with every student.

- Watch for assumptions you might make such as thinking that all students come from traditional families or that all students have parents who went to college.

- Use both the terms "he" and "she" in your lectures and correct your students when they make assumptions. Not all managers or engineers are male and not all secretaries or nurses are female.

- Be sure to call on your students equally without favoring any one age group, gender, race, or nationality.

- Give examples in class that draw from a wide range of backgrounds and cultures.

- Address inappropriate comments made by students in class that stereotype others. Take the time to make this a "teaching moment" to sensitize your students to the harm that their words and actions can do.

- Get to know the name of each student and invite them to get to know you by coming to see you during office hours.

- Encourage students with disabilities to see you so you can make accommodations to allow them to fully participate in the class.

- Ask your non-traditional students to share their work and life experiences with the other students in the classroom.

You might consider a mid-term evaluation in your classes to ask your students for their feedback on how the class is progressing, whether they feel comfortable participating (and why or why not), and whether they believe you are treating all students fairly. Below are some specific suggestions for helping all your students be more successful in the classroom.

Students with Disabilities

As part of the requirements of the Americans with Disabilities Act (ADA), professors are mandated to provide reasonable accommodations for students with disabilities.[1] In order for a student to be considered as having a disability, the ADA requires documented medical confirmation. In addition, the student must ask for accommodation in order for you to be obligated to provide it. If you have a student who is legally disabled and they do not formally request reasonable accommodation, you do not need to modify your teaching materials or methods. Most universities have an office that acquires the appropriate documentation and works with faculty in deciding what is reasonable.

Put on your syllabus that any student who feels that he or she needs a reasonable accommodation should let you know within the first few weeks of class. Your class will not be the first that the student has taken so he or she will know what it will take to function in your classroom. You are not required to grade work more leniently or compromise the academic integrity of your classes in any way.[2]

Students with disabilities also have a right to privacy. Any information about their accommodations should be kept confidential. You should not reveal or discuss a student's disability with the other students in the class.

> *I had a student who requested extra time on exams; asked to be allowed to take the exams in a separate location than the classroom; and asked to have a friend of hers read the exams to her. I was OK with the first two requests but informed her that I would provide the reader for her. While we are required to make reasonable accommodations for students with disabilities, we do not have to do everything they request. Ask yourself, would this be perceived as equitable to the other students?*
>
> **---Dr. Kirk**

Students with Visual Disabilities

Students with visual disabilities may vary from being able to read materials if the font size is large enough to not being able to see at all. Examples of reasonable accommodations might include copying handouts, quizzes, and exams in a larger font; asking for another student to volunteer to be a note taker; allowing the student to tape your lectures; and providing a scribe and extra time on exams. You might also allow a student who has a visual disability to pick a seat in the front of the classroom.

Some students will need to have the textbook and reading materials be put on tape; many universities accommodate this with student volunteers who read the materials into a tape recorder. Other students have technology such as computer software or scanners that convert materials to Braille or that read text aloud.

When using the chalkboard or whiteboard, be sure and verbalize everything that you are writing. Provide the student with any diagrams, graphics, or other visual aids you have on transparencies or Power Point slides.

Students with Hearing Disabilities
Again, students can vary in their disability from a hearing impairment to being completely deaf. Allow the student to decide where to sit. Face the student when speaking so he or she can read your lips. Make sure the student has a note-taker if requested and/or copies of your lecture notes. If the student has a sign language interpreter, make eye contact and speak to the student and not to the interpreter. If other students ask questions, repeat the question before you answer it. Also, make sure that only one person speaks at a time when conducting class discussions.

Students with Chronic Illnesses
Some students may have a chronic illness or medical disability that is difficult to ascertain from looking at them. These could include illnesses such as asthma, diabetes, cancer, and seizure disorders. On the first day of class and on your syllabus, invite your students to come see you about any medical-related academic needs. Discuss with the student what you should do in

case of an asthma attack or seizure. Work out a plan with the student in case he or she must miss classes because of hospitalization or bed rest so that the student can still get the notes and assignments. You may have to allow extra time for the student to make-up work.

> *One of my graduate students was not able to sit for any length of time because of a medical condition. We accommodated her by providing a podium at the back of the room so she could stand and take notes.*
>
> **---Dr. Kirk**

Students with Speech Impairments
Students with speech impairments are aware that others have difficulties in understanding them. Do not be afraid to ask students to repeat themselves if you do not grasp what they are saying. If necessary, ask them to write down what they are trying to say. Talk to the student about how he or she can best participate in the class. Ask if the student would be comfortable being asked questions in class or would rather write down the answer and have someone else read it. If you do call on the student, give him or her time to respond. Avoid automatically finishing the student's sentences for him or her.

Students with Learning Disabilities
You may have students in your class with a wide array of learning disabilities. These students tend to be of average or above average intelligence but have problems in processing information and thus do poorly in reading, writing, or

other academic areas. They may struggle with self-esteem and have problems with social norms and cues. The students' learning disabilities may cause them to have trouble taking notes, following instructions, completing exams timely, and organizing their time.

> *Students with learning disabilities need their professors to understand that they are not retarded or need watered-down course material. It means they are gifted in other ways. Their accommodations are no different legally than accommodating a blind or deaf student's learning needs. Students that have difficulty processing oral language may need to use tape recorders, and have directions given in writing. Other students will have difficulty processing written information and will need more info orally.*
>
> **---Anne Murr, Director**
> **Adult Literacy Center**

You can help your students with learning disabilities (and indeed all your students) by providing outlines or study guides that help point out the key concepts in the lectures or readings. Use visual aids such as white boards, overhead projectors, or Power Point slides to reinforce your lectures and class discussions. Give your assignments both orally and in writing.

If the student desires it, allow him or her to have extra time for the exams and to take these in a separate environment that is free from distractions. Give frequent feedback opportunities by offering to read drafts of papers or going over their exams question by question with your expectations. Also, put together a detailed syllabus with assignments and due dates listed. Discuss these in depth with the student at the beginning of the semester.

> *As an undergraduate, I had a college professor and advisor that called me into his office because he couldn't understand how I could get the highest score on his psychology test when according to my SAT scores I shouldn't even be in college. In fact, he told me my SAT score was equivalent to that of a "moron." At first I was thrilled that I got an "A." However, as I walked out of his office, I felt that he thought my test grade was a fluke and that I was not very intelligent after all. It had a huge impact on my self-esteem and it wasn't until ten years later that I went back to graduate school. Professors need to know that encouraging students rather than discouraging them is one of the most important influences they can have on a student's ability to succeed in anything they pursue.*
> **---Laura Walth, CHADD site facilitator and former student with AD/HD**

Age Diversity

You may have students in your classes that range from those just out of high school to workers coming back to update their skills to retirees wanting to learn more about topics of interest now that they finally have the time to explore. This could mean an age range from 18 to 60. The trick is to figure out how to motivate these different generations of college students.

Traditional Students

Today's traditional students are 18 to 22 years old and are known as Generation Y, the Millennium Generation, or the Internet Generation.[3] They have been raised in dual-income or single-parent families for the most part and thus have been given a great deal of independence and responsibility from a young age. These students tend to be multi-taskers, able to maintain conversations in several chat rooms online simultaneously while answering their ever-present cell phone. However, this dependence on technology to communicate rather than face-to-face interaction has led to a lack of what is thought of as basic social skills. Many times they do not mean to be disrespectful; they just do not understand why they cannot talk on their phone and listen to your lecture at the same time.

Be sure to establish your expectations, and communicate these expectations to the students early and often. Explain to them what a desired outcome on an assignment would look like, perhaps giving out a sample paper. Use creative ways to provide significant learning experiences through the use of cases, readings, and applications of the course content to real world situations. Realize that many of your students will be more technically competent than you are but still try to incorporate computers into your classes. Consider developing a class web site with additional information and resources for your students. These students also want immediate feedback so you might want to have a computer software package (such as Blackboard) that allows the students instant access to all grades as soon as you record them.

Generation Y students want to get to know you on a more personal basis so feel free to share stories with them in the classroom based on your own experiences. Allow them opportunities for interpersonal involvement and collaboration with their classmates. Team projects and activities are a good way to do this. Chapter 9 presents some methods of using teams. Also, if possible, give them some choice in how to do their projects and let them set their own deadlines within reason. You might give a few extra points for assignments turned in early. Make sure that the assignments are challenging and meaningful.

<u>Generation X</u>
If you had to pick the perfect student, what would he or she be like? Most of us would say we want students who are independent, able to work in teams, and are technically savvy. Generation Xers, the name given those people born between 1965 and 1980, fit that profile.[4] These are people who thrive on change. They knew more about computers by their teen years than most baby boomers will ever know. Most are hard working and pragmatic; they just think company loyalty and job security are things of the past. Financial security is very important to them and they tend to be skeptical of authority.

Many of the suggestions above for Generation Y students will work for Generation X in organizing effective learning experiences. Generation Xers love feedback. Once they get into the workforce, once a year performance appraisals will not be enough for them. They want to know what they are doing well, what they can do to improve, and what skills they should be developing. Thus, feedback should be given frequently in class. You do not need to tie grades to this but do give feedback that is specific and constructive. Help them to set goals that are challenging yet achievable and then get out of the way. Don't micromanage them but do be available for questions or concerns they may have.

Make the classroom a fun place to be. Generation Xers enjoy learning as long as they can do so in a fun atmosphere where they feel they can learn relevant new skills. Ask their opinions and show them that these count. Consider giving a open-ended questionnaire at mid-term asking them what is working well in class and what they would like to see added. Be sure and respond to their suggestions. You do not have to accept all their suggestions but show that you have read and taken these into account, tell them what you will change as well as what you cannot change and why.

Baby Boomers
These are adults born in the years 1946-1964 who have decided to come back to school, either part-time or full-time, after working many years and/or raising children. These students may use computers in their jobs but they are usually not completely comfortable with the technology and

thus are intimidated by the Generation X and Y students. They also feel at a disadvantage in the classroom as it has been many years since they have had to take notes or study for exams.

I returned to college at the age of 46 to complete a bachelor's degree I had begun at age 18. I was absolutely appalled at the behavior of my younger classmates. The thing that shocked me the most was the amount of whining the students were doing – and the willingness of many instructors to give in to their ridiculous demands. My worst experience: an economics instructor who, on the day of an exam, let the class convince him to make a 50-question multiple choice test a group project. The students wanted to collaborate with previously assigned team members and turn in only one test per group. I was flabbergasted when the instructor said that would be OK as long as no one in the class objected. I objected. Loudly. I was booed by the class. Loudly. I told them to grow up. Loudly. The instructor then said that since I had objected, we had to take the test individually. More booing ensued. He gave in. I refused to collaborate with anyone and took the test individually. When I turned in my paper, the instructor said, "I'm sorry you're upset, but what's the big deal? This isn't worth that much of your grade." My response: "You want to know what the big deal is? The big deal is that you run this class like a preschool. It's supposed to be college."

---M. Jane Harris
Penn State College of Engineering

These adult learners want to be able to take new ideas and concepts and integrate them into what they already know. They prefer classes that focus on application to real-world problems, rather than just theory. They can also bring in a wealth of work and life experiences that your traditional students will not have which makes for more interesting class sessions. They are not afraid to participate in class if encouraged. These students are usually task-oriented and highly motivated to learn. Getting full participation from Baby Boomers needs to be done in the first few weeks of class with exercises and assignments they will find useful and interesting and that allows them to invest their own experiences into the process.[5]

International Students
Realize that there are cultural differences in the education systems in other countries. This affects the concept of what it means to be a good student. In some countries, it is considered disrespectful to ask questions of your professors. It means that the professor did not do a good job explaining. In many cultures students are expected to attend lectures and take notes only. They see the professor as the expert or authority. It would be rude to interrupt or even to speak up.

Extend an invitation early in the semester to meet with your international students separately in your office. Discuss with them their assumptions and expectations. Find out what college is like in their country. Ask them if it is harder to get into an university or harder to graduate (this varies by country). Ask about the type of relationship that students in their country have with their professors. Find out how students would be evaluated or how grades are given. These questions will help you understand these international students better and open the conversation as to how expectations are different in the United States. You might also ask how they decided on their major and how this is viewed by their family. You will have students who struggle in class and when you talk with them, you will find that they were only majoring in that subject because their family insisted.

It is OK to ask a student to write something down if you are having trouble understanding him or her. Or, if you are talking to an international student on the phone, you might have him or her spell a word that you do not catch. Explain to the student that you want to communicate but that you are having trouble with his or her accent. Check to see if your university offers ESL classes or other resources that you can refer the student to for help.

Ask the student if they have trouble understanding you and what you could do in the classroom to help. Consider putting complex assignments in written format as well as giving verbal directions.

If appropriate and possible, put an international slant on an assignment so that the international students get to be the experts in class.

Students who are Academically Diverse

Your students will vary from those who are smart and highly motivated to those who find the subject difficult and were dragged into the classroom kicking and screaming. Be sure to mention the pre-requisites of the course the first day and tell students to come see you if they think they may have trouble with the course material. You might consider a pretest the first week of class to get a sense of your students' preparation for the class. Put materials on your web site or on reserve in your university library that will allow students to review knowledge or concepts they should already have in order to succeed in your class.

> *One of our students was doing poorly in his classes. When the Associate Dean called him in to talk about it, the student protested that it was not his fault. He said his roommate had a learning disability and he thought he had caught it.*
>
> **---Dr. Kirk**

The real issue will be to challenge the bright students without losing the students that are less capable. Using a variety of teaching methods and assignments will help both groups of students stay focused. Ask for feedback from your students as to what you can do to help them learn. Be aware of nonverbal cues. You can usually tell from the blank looks during the lecture that you have lost their attention. Briefly review your notes from the last class before starting the new day's lecture. Or, have the students take turns summarizing the main points in class. Make a note on the tests and papers of students who are having difficulty for them to come see you during office hours to discuss their work. Also, be available right before and after class if possible for students to ask questions. Encourage students to form study groups (or put these together for them). Give your better students the option of choosing their own paper topics.

A Final Note

Although managing a diverse classroom may be challenging, it is also rich with experiences and backgrounds that the students bring to the class. Make sure that the culture you create in the classroom is welcoming to every student. Encourage your students to get acquainted with others they might perceive as different from themselves. Create "teaching moments" to dispel stereotypes that might come up during class. Be sensitive to the time pressures that students have in attempting to juggle classes, jobs or internships, family and social life, and college activities. Make sure that the assignments you give are useful and relevant.

Dear Professor Kirk,
I cannot thank you enough, for being more than a professor to our little girl. She keeps talking about you and if there 'was' a female God, I think you would be the God as far as she is concerned. We will be coming to visit the US and it would be our privilege to meet you. Again we say thank you, thank you and thank you, for the care you have shown for our baby.
Ebu (aka Shaleen's Papa)
Mumbai, India

Questions from Faculty

Dear Dr. Kirk:

What is your perspective on why students today are disrespectful and disruptive in the classroom? Do you think that they're intentionally being rude or do they just have worse social skills than in the past?

Perplexed

Dear Perplexed,

Last Fall I did an online chat on classroom management for the *Chronicle of Higher Education* and afterwards I received hundreds of e-mails from professors all over the United States that are having issues with disruptive behaviors in the classroom. There is obviously a change in student behavior in the past few years. I think part of the problem is a lack of role models. There appears to be a general lack of civility in the "real world" and this trickles down to the educational system. Students see inappropriate behavior and disrespect for others in businesses, churches, and the government. When was the last time you were in a meeting and someone's cell phone rang? It happened here at a faculty meeting.

I also think the emphasis that many universities have on the student as the "customer" contributes. Faculty are afraid of making the students upset as this reflects on tenure, promotion, and salary decisions. If we don't stand up to our students and tell them no, why would we think it would occur to them that their behavior might be rude?

Don't get me wrong. I don't think students are bad. I just think that we, as professors, need to establish our expectations for acceptable behavior. I find that if I set classroom policies on tardiness, attendance, late papers, etc and convey my expectations to my students, they are more than willing to accept these rules. An important part of that is enforcing the policies fairly and consistently. I present it to the students that when they get that "first real job" after college, it would be useful to know their bosses' pet peeves.

Dear Dr. Kirk:
I have a student from another country that thinks I should grade his papers more leniently because English is not his first language. What do I tell him?

Trying to Do the Right Thing

Dear Trying,
I appreciate your sensitivity. Coming to another country and attending classes taught in a foreign language has to be difficult. However, his diploma will not say on it that it is a "lenient" degree for students for which English is not their home language. If he wants a degree from an university in the United States, he has to complete the same requirements as all the other students.

Comments from Students

Coming to America was an cultural shock to me; My 4 months' experience here tells me that to understand of my peers' fast and vague pronunciations is a real challenge to me. I also had an experience with a retailer store "American" when I ordered some home appliances as (1) I was forced to follow their delivery schedule; (2) When I cancelled $1,000 (1/3 of my order) easily without receiving any solicitation to keep it or any alternative proposals from the staff; (3) When I received a big table unassembled.

I am at your disposal, ByeongHo
Student from South Korea

Firstly, this is wishing you a very Happy New Year. Its a pleasure for me to speak as part of your book. This is the least I can do for you, as a student. Please inform me what you want me to address specifically in the discussion, so I can prepare myself. I also would like to request you to please keep a seat in front for me in the classroom, as I am very comfortable ahead, in all classes. I would appreciate it if you could please acknowledge the receipt of this e-mail. I would also ask you to inform me if you want me to bring anything from Bombay and/or India, that would help me to make the presentation a more informative and fun one. Looking forward to hearing from you again, replying to the above questions and concerns.

Thanking you, Aditya
Student from India

Endnotes:

[1]Americans with Disabilities Act, www.eeoc.gov/policy/ada.html

[2]www.adapts.gatech.edu/faculty_guide/teach.htm;

[3]www.as.wvu.edu/scidis/learning.html

[4]www.royalneighbors.com/virtual_community/askthepanel/index.cfm

[5]Kirk, Delaney J., "Generation X Workers Can Be Motivated With These Three Steps," *Des Moines Register*, June 26, 2000.

[6]Zemke, Ron, and Susan Zemke, "30 Things We Know for Sure About Adult Learning," *Innovation Abstracts*, March 19, 1984; Thoms, Karen Jarett, "They're Not Just Big kids: Motivating Adult Learners," at www.mtsu.edu/~itconf/proceed01/22.pdf

CHAPTER 7

Managing Difficult Students

*People's behavior makes sense
if you think about it in terms of
their goals, needs, and motives.*

---Thomas Mann

Teaching has become more challenging in the past few years because college students have become more aggressive and demanding. Inappropriate student behavior has become such a serious issue that schools such as the University of Arizona have developed a video of "bad classroom behavior" that they show to all their incoming freshmen.[1]

My first introduction to this aggression in students was in an Operations Management class. I had given the students a problem to work on and one of the students had finished hers and raised her hand to ask me to check her answer. I showed her my paper with the problem and answer on it. The answer differed from hers. Instead of assuming that she had done the problem incorrectly, she got very belligerent and announced that MY answer must be wrong.

---Dr. Kirk

Chapter 1 of this book discusses the process of determining your classroom policies in order to establish the classroom culture that you want. Chapter 2 advocates putting those polices in writing in your syllabus and Chapters 3 and 4 discuss communicating these to your students on the first day of class. The task that follows is enforcing and reinforcing these policies for the rest of the semester. This includes dealing with students who fail to adhere to the rules you have set. You may have clearly thought out the expectations that were communicated to your students, but everything hinges on how you deal with those students who ignore your policies, whether aggressively or passively.

In his research on effective and ineffective classroom managers, Jacob Kounin found that the most effective teachers have something he called, "*withitness.*"[2] A teacher with "*withitness*" is not only cognizant of what the students are doing in the classroom, the students are also aware that the teacher knows. Unfortunately, professors tend to ignore inappropriate behavior from students for many reasons including they:

- Have not been taught the skills necessary to handle behavioral issues.

- Are not sure that their chair or dean will support their actions if a student files a complaint.

- Feel guilty disciplining others when they did the same thing as a student.

- Note that their colleagues do not seem to care if students or sleeping in class or coming to class tardy.

- Do not want others to know they are having problems controlling their classroom.

- Believe it takes valuable time to deal with behavioral issues with students.

- Are afraid of getting angry or upset when confronting a disruptive student.

- Believe that the student knows to come to class on time so why talk about it?

- Want their students to like them.

However, according to Kounin, "how a teacher handles one student's misbehavior influences the other students who are not misbehaving," something he termed the "Ripple Effect."[3] Thus, the rest of the class is looking to see whether you enforce your own policies. In order to handle difficult students and prevent the Ripple Effect, be proactive in addressing issues that come up in the classroom.

There are several categories of difficult students. These include students who are disruptive, not engaged in the class, break the class rules, or are confused about the course expectations. Some students may fit into more than one category. The following are specific examples of these types of students as well as suggestions for working with them with the goal of fostering an ideal classroom environment.

> *On the first day of class I ask my students to share their experiences of disruptive behavior that they have seen in other classes. Peer pressure is a useful tool in establishing guidelines in the classroom. If you set and communicate policies regarding tardiness or cell phone use, you will see the other students turn around and look at the student who is late or whose phone rings.*
>
> **---Dr. Kirk**

Disruptive students
Disruptive students disturb the flow of the classroom. These students hog the class discussion, challenge you as the professor, whine about assignments and exams, or talk to others nearby while you're lecturing.

<u>The Class Hog</u>
Actually the student who always has something to say is a valuable asset during the first few weeks of class. When you ask a question of the class, you hope someone will respond. However, at some point this student begins inhibiting the other students from participating. You may even notice other students rolling their eyes whenever the Class Hog begins to speak.

One way to handle the Class Hog is to thank the student in class for participating and then say you want to hear ideas and perspectives from others who do not usually speak up. If you give participation points as part of the grade, you can use that to justify calling on others. Require students to raise their hands to comment or answer questions. Make eye contact with another student and move toward him or her. Consider giving the Class Hog a role such as recording the suggestions to a question or problem posed by you. Or, involve the class members by asking them what could be done in class to ensure everyone gets a chance to participate. Keep in mind that Class Hogs need attention and consider giving the student individual time outside of class.

> *A technique I have used to deal with students that hog the class discussion is to pass out three poker chips per student. Each student has to use these up by the end of class so the quieter ones must participate while the vocal ones have to limit their comments.*
>
> **---Dave Bloomquist**
> **University of Florida**

The Challenger
The Challenger is the student who is always challenging you as the professor. Establishing your credibility the first day of class will help alleviate the situation. If the Challenger asks you a pointed question while in the classroom, try redirecting it back to him or her or to other students in the class. If the student persists in disagreeing with your point, say that you will have to "agree to disagree on that issue." Another approach might be to get acquainted with the Challenger on a one-on-one basis outside of class.

Getting to know the student on a more personal level may help them "buy into" the class. Ask the student about his or her background and future career plans. Show that you respect the student as an individual and that you want to help in the learning process. However, if the negative behavior continues, make it clear to the student that the disrespect has to stop. Most students will back down at this point when they realize that you are aware of their disruptive behavior.

> *I had a student who had a bad attitude in class and was extremely hostile toward me. I finally confronted her (later than I should have) and asked her to talk to me outside. I think she was expecting to get thoroughly scolded. I remained very calm and simply stated: "You seem very frustrated. What is bothering you?" She told me that she felt that the class was too easy for her, and that it was annoying to have to sit through it. I told her that I would be happy if she took the placement test again and tried to test out of the class. But I also told her firmly that the negative and disrespectful attitude was inappropriate and had to stop. I told her that if she continued to be in my class, that she had to participate courteously. I had to talk to her one more time after that, but I feel that talking to her as an adult and acknowledging her feelings were important—it surprised her and in some way earned me some respect.*
> ---**Paula Thonney**
> **Brookdale Community College**

The Whiner

There will always be students who complain about the workload, their grades, the tests, etc. Part of being proactive in handling the whiners is to explain early in the semester how the assignments will benefit them in their future careers or lives. If you do assign a lot of homework, make sure that these are useful assignments to understanding the course material.

If students whine in class, tell them that this is not the time or place to make changes in classroom policies or assignments. You might also try validating the student's point. For example, say, "yes, I understand that there is a lot of work due in the next week. What resources can I share with you to help?" Tell the student you would be happy to meet with them during your office hours to discuss their concerns.

I attended a teaching workshop where the presenter talked about her method of dealing with student whining. She told her students that if they don't complain about tests or paper grades during the semester, they would get an extra five points at the end. They are allowed to come in and tell her if she made a mistake but not to whine just because they didn't like their grade. She said she found that this cuts out most of the whining. I myself have even gone so far as to directly ask the student, "Are you whining?" or "Would you like some cheese with that whine?"

---Dr. Kirk

The Socializer
Socializers disrupt the classroom by talking to nearby students while you are lecturing. This is annoying to other students in class who are attempting to listen and take notes.

One way to handle The Socializer is to stop and ask if he or she has a question or needs you to clarify something. You could also try moving slowly toward those who are talking as you continue to lecture. If you don't want to embarrass or directly confront the students talking, ask a student sitting near The Socializer a question. Another tactic is to stop lecturing, make eye contact with The Socializers, and wait for the talking to cease. Usually peer pressure from others in class will help enforce that The Socializer needs to be quiet. Another suggestion would be to move The Socializer to another seat closer to you in front.

> *On occasion I have asked a group of students to stay after class and explained to them that I don't mind a little discussion on the side, but if it is so loud that I really notice it, then it is disruptive to the class and they need to stop. This is best to do early in the semester. If you allow the talking to continue for several weeks, you've essentially said it's ok with you.*
>
> **---Dr. Kirk**

Non-engaged Students
Some students rarely, if ever, participate in class discussions. This may be due to shyness or to cultural differences. Others are simply unpre-

pared for class and thus have nothing to contribute. Still others do not seem to understand the relevance of the class to them and thus are simply "warm bodies" waiting for the semester to be over.

The Shy Student

You will have some students that are just shy. Others are afraid to speak up fearing that they may have the wrong answer. However, since you do not let students opt out of taking exams or writing papers, you should insist on their active participation as part of the learning process. It is necessary to create a classroom culture where everyone's opinion is valid and the students do not have to fear that you or the other students will make fun of them.

You may have international students who come from educational systems where it is considered disrespectful to ask questions. In some countries, questioning the professor meant the student is saying that the professor did not explain the concept well. You will have to let them know you want their feedback and encourage them to participate. More suggestions on involving the international student are included in Chapter 6 on Managing Diversity in the Classroom.

Give the Shy Student a "heads-up" that you will be calling on him or her later so it does not come as a surprise. Be sure and give positive reinforcement for any type of effort or comment made by the student. Consider making the Shy Student the leader of a small group discussion in which you give the class a question and a couple of minutes to write down their answer. Ask the Shy Student to read the group's answer from that paper.

> *I put my students into teams of four. I give each person on the team the same number but from a different suit of a deck of cards. I then rotate leadership within the teams by announcing that today, "the diamonds are the spokespersons."*
> **---John Cox**
> **Ouachita Baptist University**

The Unprepared Student
Dealing with the Unprepared Student is simply a matter of establishing accountability. If you give assignments that you do not collect or discuss in class, the Unprepared Student thinks that it is OK not to do these. Address this issue early in the semester by giving an assignment on the first day for the next class meeting. Students will then see that you consider the assignments important and relevant. You do not have to give quizzes every class period; in fact, give them randomly so that the students feel that they always need to be prepared.

Consider giving points that are based on your assignments as part of the class grade; be sure and explain to the students how you will grade these. Also, try tying your lecture to the assignments by mentioning a specific page in the textbook or something from the article the students were supposed to read so that they can see the connection. The key to managing Unprepared

Students is letting them know you will be holding them accountable for their work.

The Clueless Student

Some students will not recognize the relevance of the class to them. This lack of understanding becomes especially obvious in those classes that are not specific to their major but are instead required to be taken by all students. It is up to the professor to explain why these classes are important and how they fit into the Clueless Student's education.

> *On the first day of class, I share my varied career history with the students to illustrate that I had no idea at 18 or 20 years old what would be useful to me later either in my career or life.*
> ---**Dr. Kirk**

One approach to demonstrating relevancy is to ask the students what they are majoring in and then tying the class material to those careers during the semester. You should discuss with the students that people tend to have a number of different careers during their work history so it is difficult to tell what will be relevant later. In addition, explain to the students that a well-rounded person knows about many things other than their major in college. Having guest speakers in class who talk about their career decisions and what they wished they had paid more attention to in class is an excellent way to get the Clueless Student's attention.

The Rule Breakers

Rule Breakers refuse to follow classroom policies on attendance, tardiness, sleeping in class, cell phone use, reading newspapers, turning in papers late, and cheating.

> *I insist that they don't eat, drink, chew, or wear hats in class, and I've become a stickler for punctuality with assignments. We can't reform human nature, obviously, but to some extent we can adapt it. I've found my students' hunger for good grades makes them willing to fall in with my demands.*
>
> **---Patrick Allitt**
> **Emory University**

The Absent or Tardy Student

The best way to deal with the Absent or Tardy Student is to have your policy spelled out on your syllabus. Share this policy and your expectations on the first day of class. Explain to the students that they will be required to go to work every day and on time when they get into the workforce and that you are helping them role model these behaviors.

> *I give my students two "personal" days that they can use to miss class for any reason. This allows students to miss up to two quizzes without penalty which makes my policy seem fair to them without my having to make judgment calls on the students' excuses for absences.*
>
> **---Dr. Kirk**

Just as managers can't make their employees do anything in the workplace, you cannot make the students come to class every day on time. But you can set consequences and enforce these; be sure to be consistent in applying the rules. During the first couple weeks of classes, pull any Tardy Student aside after class and ask the student if he or she knows what the policy is on tardiness. Remind the student that coming to class on time is part of the requirements of the class. If students come in late and you do not address the issue either immediately or after class, you have essentially said the tardiness is OK. If you do not handle this issue early in the semester, you will find other students will begin to come in tardy also.

Another method to help motivate the Tardy Student to come to class on time is to give random pop quizzes at the beginning of the class. You could use these quizzes as a way of taking attendance. This will also help motivate the Absent Student if you do not allow makeups for these quizzes; they must be present and on time to take the quiz.

Another way of handling the Tardy Student is to wait until he or she is seated and then ask a question, possibly dealing with the assignment due for the day. The Tardy Student will quickly make the connection that he or she will be singled out if late to class.

The Sleeper

Some professors are not bothered by Sleepers but again you should consider that you are role modeling professional behavior in the workplace. These students will not be allowed to keep their jobs if they sleep at work.

Try standing near The Sleeper and continue to lecture, raising your voice slightly. Call on a student next to the sleeping student and ask him or her a question. Or, call on the sleeping student; be prepared to repeat your question. Talk to The Sleeper after class and ask why he or she cannot stay awake and what could be done to improve the situation. Keep in mind that you do need to make the class interesting if you want to keep all the students engaged and awake.

In my "Class from Hell," I had a student that fell asleep during every class period. I tried all of the above suggestions but nothing was working. I could see that the other students were watching to see how I would handle the situation. Finally one day I woke "Bob" up, told him I was very concerned about his health as I had noticed him falling asleep in class. I directed him to get his books and report to the Student Health Center. He tried to tell me that he wasn't sick but I insisted, said that I couldn't live with myself if he was truly sick with a serious illness and I hadn't gotten him medical help. Bob sheepishly left the room and never slept in my class again.

---Dr. Kirk

The Cell Phone User

You may need to remind the students every class period for the first few weeks to turn off their phones or beepers. If someone's phone does ring, make a small joke about it such as, "That's a nice phone but please turn it off" or "Is that for me?" Humor will make your point for most students. You will also find that the other students will turn around and glare at The Cell Phone User if they know your rule about turning the phone off before class. Again, peer pressure is always a powerful tool.

The Reader

One student who is discreetly reading a newspaper or doing work for another class does not bother some professors. However, you should keep in mind that the other students are watching to see how you handle The Reader. Soon you will have two students reading the paper. Talk to The Reader after class and tell him or her that you find the behavior disrespectful to you and to the other students. Ask The Reader to refrain from doing unrelated activities in the future. Also, note in the syllabus your expectations for the use of class time.

The Late Paper

Research shows that two-thirds of students have admitted to making at least one false excuse during their college career.[4] Again, it helps to have a written policy in the syllabus as to how you will handle any late papers or assignments. Discuss this policy the first day of class and give several reminders in class of upcoming deadlines. Build in accountability for the students. For example, have students turn in an outline of their paper or a list of references they will be using several weeks before the paper is due.

When asked by students for extra time to complete an assignment, explain to them that it is not fair to their classmates for them to have more time to do research and writing. This justifies your deducting points for past due assignments.

You will need to decide what your policy is for The Late Paper. You could refuse to accept late papers and assignments but be sure and spell this out in your syllabus. There will be extreme cases such as a car accident, serious illness, or a death in the family where you may decide on a case-by-case basis to waive your policy. However, consider these carefully and make sure you have verification of the emergency situation.

You could also consider a bonus for papers turned in early to help motivate students.

> *I usually accept late papers but with a penalty; I subtract 10% of the final grade after the first 24 hours and another 10% after each additional day. I also set a deadline, usually one week, after which I will not accept the paper.*
> **---Dr. Kirk**

The Cheater
The Cheater has wandering eyes during exams, plagiarizes on papers, or may even purchase re-

search papers to use as his or her own. Chapter 8 on Managing Exams presents some methods of handling potential cheating on tests.

It is best to be proactive in preventing cheating on papers and assignments. Let your students know that you expect them to do their own work and that cheating will be punished in your class. Put your policy on cheating (or your university's policy) in your syllabus. You should also be familiar with your university's procedures on reporting cheating so that you follow the appropriate steps if this becomes necessary.

Define the term plagiarism for your students. Many of them do not understand the difference between citing and copying someone else's work. Give specific and timely topics on papers so that The Cheater cannot simply access the internet for commercially produced papers. Have students turn in outlines and/or first drafts of their papers to you earlier in the semester and then have them attach those drafts to the final paper when it is due. Also, require them to turn in copies of all sources cited including web sites, journal articles, and pages of books used.

There are web sites that help faculty identify plagiarized papers. The technology allows faculty to submit student papers through a web site. The papers are then compared against a database of materials from books, journals, and web pages on the Internet. There is typically a cost for this service and individual instructors, departments, or universities can subscribe to the service.[5]

> *I had a student falsify an assignment in which he was supposed to interview a manager and write a paper on what he had learned. When he challenged the zero grade I gave him, I simply handed him information on the appeal process, reminding him that in order to appeal, both his coach and the dean of the college would have to be notified as to what he had done. He took the zero.*
>
> **---Dr. Kirk**

The Confused Student

Some of your students will do the work assigned but will have difficulty with the material or will not understand what is expected of them.

When giving back quizzes or exams, invite the Confused Student who has not done as well as he or she would have liked to come see you in your office. Consider writing the comment, "Come see me about this grade" on his or her paper.

Ask the Confused Student why he or she thinks the grade was lower than expected. Inquire about study habits and attendance. Ask to see class notes and make suggestions on how these could be improved. The practice of recopying notes after class, or at least before the next class, will help to jog the Confused Student's memory. This activity will also help the Confused Student identify areas he or she does not understand. You might also suggest the student meet with others in the class and form a study group. See Figure 2.1 in Chapter 2 for tips for success you could adapt for your students.

A Final Note

Most students will respond to your request that they follow the class policies as long as you treat them with respect. Addressing issues one-on-one allows them to keep their dignity. It is best to handle inappropriate behaviors the same day that they occur. Otherwise, the students will think it is OK to break your rules.

Point out the inappropriate behavior and remind him or her of the class policy. Stay calm and do not take the situation personally; be matter of fact about your expectations for the future. Keep in mind your rationale for the rules you have established and the impact that inappropriate behavior has in the classroom. You are trying to be corrective and not punitive. Afterwards, document the issue and your actions. Keep a written record of students, policies not followed, and what you said and did. This provides you with an accurate accounting of the steps you took to resolve the situation and provides back-up in case you have to justify your actions. If you are not sure how to handle a situation, seek the advice of colleagues or your department chair or dean.

In extreme cases, remember that you always have recourse if things really get out of hand. Contact your security department, or even the police, if an disruptive student is aggressive and refuses to leave the class.

Once I made the mistake of getting very angry at a student in class. He got very upset and said something rude back to me. I then told him he had to stay after class. I think he was extremely agitated, angry, and nervous, and he didn't stay. The following day, I again asked him to stay after class and he seemed a little calmer but still considerably agitated. I simply said to him, "I'm sorry. I shouldn't have gotten so angry with you." He was so relieved and immediately said that he was sorry for being rude. After that we got along very well. I think he respected me for being able to back down.

---**Paula Thonney**
Brookdale Community College

Questions from Faculty

Dear Dr. Kirk:
Recently, one of my students came to me complaining about another student, "Bob." According to the student, Bob has such an offensive body odor that students don't want to sit next to him and his team doesn't want to work with him. This is the first time I've encountered a problem like this and I really don't know how to handle it. What should I do?

Awkward in Boise

Dear Awkward,
This is one of those situations where a professor really gets to earn his or her pay. Your first instinct may be to either ignore the problem or to confront Bob and tell him to take a shower. However, there are a number of issues here that you should consider before talking to Bob.

Ignoring the problem probably won't make it go away. However, before taking any steps, you need to verify the accuracy of the complaint. It could be that the other students just don't like Bob and want to embarrass him. Ask Bob to see you after class and make your own first hand observation to make sure there really is a problem. You want to be sure that the student who complained to you didn't have an ulterior motive.

Be aware that the body odor issue could be covered by state or federal discrimination laws. For example, the odor could be caused by a medical condition and thus fall under the Americans with Disabilities Act. Or, it may be the result of an ethnic diet which could be covered by Title VII of the Civil Rights Act. Don't make assumptions as to what is causing the body odor. For example, don't assume that it is the person's diet and ask that Bob change his eating habits.

If you have determined that there is a body odor problem, approach the student with tact but state the facts. Tell the student he has a problem that is affecting others and that you expect him to take care of it. Be sympathetic but direct. Conduct the conversation one-on-one in your office or in a private area. Do ask for suggestions on what Bob thinks he could do to solve the problem. Perhaps he is coming straight to class from working out at the gym and could reschedule his exercise time. Be sure and check up afterwards to make sure the problem is solved and that the students are not teasing Bob.

Although problems like this may be embarrassing to deal with, they are more common that many people realize and can range from heavy perspiration odors, lack of regular bathing, or too much perfume. Many times the student doesn't realize that the problem exists until confronted. Thus, it's important to preserve the student's dignity and handle the issue with tact.

Dear Dr. Kirk:
I've heard you talk about how to get the shy student to participate in class but as long as the student is paying attention, is it necessary to get them to participate?

Shy Myself in College

Dear Shy,
I believe it *is* important. Obviously, shy students will always have shyness as part of their personality makeup but they can learn to become more comfortable in presenting their opinions and concerns. Even if they choose a job that does not require interaction with customers, they will need to share their ideas with their co-workers and boss on occasion. In addition, they will need to interact with their children's teachers, their church or civic groups, etc. Learning how to participate is a skill that anyone can learn.

Dear Dr. Kirk:
What happens when a student complains about you to your chair or dean and they do not realize that a student is disruptive in class and takes the student's side?

Who's in Charge Here Anyway?

Dear In Charge,
Tell the chair or dean you would like their advice as to how to handle disruptive students and invite him or her to sit in on your class.

Comments from Students

I hate teachers that talk down to students; respect us and our age, I am not 5.

Angie

I had a tax accounting professor a year and a half ago who said he was a "bad ass" and that he would tell the government to go screw themselves. I thought this was inappropriate behavior.

Heidi

My worse professor would talk about places he had been that would have nothing to do with the class just to show how "great" he was. I stopped going to class because I could not stand him and my grade improved because I studied from the book and then just went to class when there were tests.

Kane

I tend to associate bad teachers with not being able to make the class interesting and fun, which tends to be the classes I got the worst grades in because I tend to zone out and lose interest. Professors should be passionate about their classes to make them interesting.

Mathew

Endnotes:

[1]Young, Jeffrey R., "Sssshhh. We're Taking Notes Here: Colleges Look for New Ways to Discourage Disruptive Behavior in the Classroom," *Chronicle of Higher Education,* August 8, 2003.

[2]Kounin, J. S., *Discipline and Group Management in Classrooms.* New York: Holt, Rinehart and Winston,1970.

[3]Same as (2)

[4]Caron, M.D., S. Whitbourne, and R. Halgin, "Fradulent Excuse Making Among College Students, *Teaching of Psychology*, 19(2), 1992.

[5]Turnitin.com is one of the web sites that investigates whether papers are plagerized.

CHAPTER 8

Managing Exams

*If you can't explain it simply, you
don't understand it well enough.*
---Albert Einstein

One of the least enjoyable, but necessary, tasks
of a professor is to evaluate students' performance, usually in the form of exams. You will
have to decide what type of exams to give, how to
handle requests for make-up exams, and how to
prevent cheating on examinations. Students will
disagree with your grading and beg or demand
additional points. In this chapter are suggestions for handling these issues as well as ideas
for what you can do to help students improve
their performance on future exams.

Before the Exam
Stress on the first day of class, and in your syllabus, the importance of taking exams at the designated time and date. Plan examination dates
before classes begin and tell your students so
that they can put these on their calendar. It
is better to test on less material if you are not
able to cover everything you had planned than
it is to change exam dates. Decide on the type
of examinations you will give and build grading
time into your own calendar so you can get the

results back to students as quickly as possible. Timely feedback is one of the criteria on teaching evaluations at many universities.

> *I like to spread out the workload based on my class schedule. For example, when I'm teaching a class that meets on Tuesdays and Thursdays, I will schedule an exam on Thursday so I have the weekend to grade and can get results back the following Tuesday. This helps to convince the students that I am organized and that teaching is a priority for me.*
>
> **---Dr. Kirk**

Make-up Exam Policies

Scheduling time for both the student and professor to be available for the make-up exam can be a problem. If you decide to put together a new examination, it will take additional time and there is the concern that it is not comparable. If you use the original, there is the very real possibility that the other students have divulged information about the exam.

Require your students to notify you prior to the test period if they have to miss an exam due to an illness or last minute emergency. You could allow them to e-mail you or leave a phone message. Have a policy stating that the make-up must be completed within a specified time frame at your convenience. Possible make-up exam policies could include:

- Giving several exams throughout the semester and letting the students drop their lowest score. If they miss an exam, that is the one that will be dropped

- Schedule make-up exams to take place after the final is given during Finals Week. This can be a deterrent not to miss the originally scheduled exam.

- Count one of the other exams twice to make-up for the missing exam. You will have to decide which one. Some professors count the final twice.

Type of Exam

Another decision to make is the type of exam you will give your students. As mentioned earlier, prompt feedback is very important to your students so choose the type of exam you give with a quick turnaround goal in mind. Try to aim for the very next class period. It is admirable to give full essay exams if you can get these graded quickly. If you cannot, consider a test that is part objective and part essay. If you give fill in the blank questions, be sure to include a list of terms or you will have students making up their own words.

Develop two or more versions of the exam and switch the order of the questions. If the test is multiple-choice format, you might put the answers in a different order. Make the cover sheet of the exam a different color for each version so students are well aware that there is more than one test.

Extra Credit

Consider including a two point extra credit question at the end of an exam to give the students a chance for additional points. When giving back the exams, you can then point out that you do this in case one or two of the objective questions are a little unclear for them. This opportunity for extra credit on the exam will help eliminate whining or requests for partial credit.

Review for the Exam

Some professors set aside a day to review for exams. Others review notes from the previous class at the beginning of each new class. You might suggest students form study groups and develop their own exam questions to use in quizzing each other. If a great deal of material is covered on the exam, the students will be very appreciative if you put together a study sheet for them. Consider making copies of old tests available on either your web site or on reserve in your university library. During the week before the exam, write your office hours on the board and tell the students to start studying early so they can come see you with any questions they might have. See Figure 2.1 in Chapter 2 for tips for studying you could adapt for your students.

> *I include the study sheet for the final on my syllabus. The students can check off what they have learned throughout the semester and be ready for the comprehensive final exam.*
> **---Dr. Kirk**

During the Exam

It takes two things for students to be able to cheat: motivation and opportunity. While you cannot affect someone's motivation to cheat, you can take away the opportunity.

Either proctor the exam yourself or make sure that whoever is proctoring for you remains in the room at all times. Stand in the back of the room so the students cannot see if you are watching.

In large classes, or situations where you do not know the students by sight, consider checking their photo IDs before giving them the exam. If the room is large enough, have the students spread out and leave an empty chair between each other.

If you suspect that a student is cheating during an exam, go and stand near the student or ask the student to move to another seat, stating that it is a little crowded where he or she is sitting and you want to give the student more room. Do not accuse him or her of cheating but make the student aware that you are watching.

Consider keeping all copies of the exams so you can use portions of these in other semesters and not have to worry about sorority or fraternity "test banks." You can give students the option of coming to your office to look at these again if you have a comprehensive final.

I was proctoring an exam and stepped out of the room for two minutes. After class I received a phone call from a student who told me that two students were looking at each other's exams while I was gone. She was not willing to make a formal statement. After getting over my initial anger, I developed the scenario in Figure 8.1 and put the class into teams to discuss during the next class period. In this scenario, applicants for a job cheated on an employment test. My students were very upset about the cheating and recommended that none of the applicants be hired. I then explained what happened without using names and we had a "teaching moment" on the impact of cheating. Students are sometimes OK with others cheating on exams but get upset when you explain that that person might get the job they wanted due to a higher GPA because of cheating.

---Dr. Kirk

Grading Exams

While grading exams, pay careful attention to any question missed by many of the students. It is very likely they will ask about that question when you give the exam back so you want to make sure that the wording is clear to you. Be proactive and announce in class that a number of students missed the question and then discuss why you consider each of the incorrect answers to be wrong. Or, you may decide that the question was poorly worded and throw it out or give credit for it regardless of the answer.

When grading essay questions, it helps to deveop a rubric for how you plan to grade. Decide on the main points you want the students to cover and how much each is worth. Give the students enough feedback on the essay so that they can see what was missed and why.

Issues you will run into if you teach quantitative courses is that the students will want partial credit for problems that they felt were "partially correct." For example, students will make a serious math error but insist that they understand the problem. Try dividing up the problem into smaller sections and allocate fewer points to each. Another solution to this conflict is to take a number of old exams, look at the types of incorrect answers the students tend to get, and put those problems into a multiple-choice format. The students still have to work the problems but then must indicate which answer they got.

> *I had a lot of whining for partial credit until I started putting the answers to the problems into multiple-choice format. I find I no longer have requests for partial credit even though the problems I use are the same as before.*
> **---Dr. Kirk**

Returning Exams
When you return the exams, write the overall distribution of the test on the board. Students like to see where they stand in comparison to their classmates. Include the mean, median, highest score, and the number received of each

letter grade.   Some professors also include the lowest score but others believe this is demoralizing to the student who did so poorly. If you have more than one section of the class, indicate how the other class compared.

If it is an objective or partial objective exam, you could go through the answers very quickly in class to reassure students that these were marked correctly. If it is an essay exam, briefly discuss your expectations for each section. Or, consider reading an example of a good answer (without identifying the student).

Do not get into an argument with a student over an exam question in class. You will find the other students backing that student up. Tell the students to come see you during office hours if they have individual questions about their exam.

> *I usually give exams back during the last few minutes of class as I find the students want to spend less time going over it than if I return the exam at the beginning of class.*
>
> **---Dr. Kirk**

Additional Learning Opportunities
Obviously we want our students to learn from their testing experiences and be able to improve on future exams. Consider giving the exam back to your students with the incorrect questions circled but without the correct answer indicated. Use the following steps to help the students learn from their mistakes.

- Have the students go through and see if they can figure out the correct answer.

- See if the students can determine if the exam questions missed came from your lecture, the textbook, readings, class discussions, or other information.

- Have the students note why they think they missed each question. Was it due to missing class and not having complete notes, a careless mistake, something in your lecture they did not really understand, or test anxiety?

- Ask the students to look for a pattern in why they missed certain questions.

- Have the students think about what they will do differently to study for the next exam.

You might give a few extra points for this process or just explain that this will pay off for them on the next exam.

Sometimes I put the students into groups and let them take the objective part of the test again. It is the same exam but I haven't given back the original one yet so they don't know how they did. Depending on how well the groups do, the students can earn additional points that will then be added to their individual exam scores. This usually doesn't take any longer than going over the test and the students learn from each other. —***Dr. Kirk***

Student Complaints

One way to handle complaints about exams is to require that any questions that the students have be submitted to you in writing. Most students will not take the time to do this or will realize why they missed the question when they research it. Be sure to put a deadline on the acceptance of these written requests. You could develop a form for the students to use. Require them to type out the original question, explain why they think the question was poorly written, and then write a better question.

If students do come to see you in your office to talk about their exam, let them present their case without interruption, except perhaps to clarify a point. Listen carefully to why they disagree with how you graded their exam. However, you do not want to reward for good negotiation skills. Decide whether they have a valid point or if they are simply trying to get you to change their grade. Shift the discussion from the present exam to what they could do to improve for the next one. Inquire about their study habits, how they felt they did after they left the exam, and what they would do differently to study the next time. Suggest they get a study partner or that they make-up note cards with questions on one side and the answers on the other. Ask them to bring in their notes so that you can see if they are getting the main points during lecture. Show the students that you are there to help them earn a better grade next time but that you are not going to "give away" points. You do not want to get a reputation as someone who can be talked into a higher exam score or you will have many more students in your office negotiating for points.

> *To ensure that I am not rewarding for negotiation skills, I let my students know that I have been putting together exams for a long time and that it is very rare for me to change a grade unless I made a mistake marking the exam. Establishing this upfront sends the student the message that they cannot "talk you" into a better grade.*
> **---Dr. Kirk**

A Note on Homework
Professors tend to grade easier on homework than on exams because homework is not worth as many points. It can also take a lot of time to grade. However, this causes the students to slack off, be sloppy, or not do the homework at all. Grade homework thoroughly so the students know your expectations. Otherwise, when they make the same mistakes on a timed exam and lose points, they will view the exam as unfair.

A Final Note
Consider asking your students for feedback after your first exam. Tell the students to consider it a letter to you about how things are going in the class. Ask questions about the test and how useful the homework was. Take these up, read them, and write responses back. The students will appreciate being able to give feedback as well as getting your suggestions for their future success in the class.

Figure 8.1: Case on Cheating

In your teams, read the following scenario and decide what you would do as the manager.

Your company has a opening for an entry-level job. You have gone through the recruiting process and identified a group of 30 qualified applicants. As part of your selection process, you administer an employment test. All 30 applicants took the test yesterday at the company's testing site. This morning you find out from two different applicants (who seek you out separately) that there were a couple of people who cheated on the test while the proctor was briefly out of the room. You did not see this yourself and thus have no proof. What do you do?

Questions from Faculty

Dear Dr. Kirk:
What if you really believe in essay question tests but can't get these graded and back to the students within your "next class" requirement?

Slow but Careful Grader

Dear Grader,
The students will understand as long as you give them a date by which to expect the feedback on the test. When I take up something that will take longer to grade such as an essay exam or research paper, I always give them a date to expect the exam or paper back, usually two weeks away. As long as I meet that deadline, the students will be OK with the delay. If possible, I try to get the results back to them a little earlier which really impresses them.

Dear Dr. Kirk:
How do you deal with a student who insists on discussing a test question with you during the class period? I don't mind taking some time in class to go over the exam but many times these students are disrespectful and don't get, or want to get, the feedback I'm trying to give them.

Frustrated Test Giver

Dear Frustrated,
I would invite them to come to my office during office hours to discuss the question but tell them that right now I need to cover the material that will be on their next test!

Comments from Students

My political science professor taught class which consisted of trying to write down every word he said because he required essay answers to be said nearly word for word on the test. Tests reflected memorization over understanding. Original thinking seemed discouraged; he didn't seem to care about student learning.

Marc

I had a professor for an introductory finance class who required that we memorize all the formulas for the test. Also, he just read the Power Point slides to us and didn't apply them.

Tyler

The worse instructor I had was not prepared for class and did not give back grades or respond to how I was doing on homework. I never knew how I was doing grade-wise so that I could try to improve.

Brett

I had an accounting professor who tested the class on material that didn't resemble any of the homework or lectures. His reasoning was as follows, "When it comes to accounting in the real world, you will be given receipts, notes, books, etc. Never in text book format, so you must know what to do." I agree with this to a certain point, but I think most companies will have "templates" or some type of format to follow.

Lisa

CHAPTER 9

Managing Teams and Team Projects

The teaching goes on.
---Mitch Albom

Many professors use some type of team learning in their classrooms as they realize that students need to learn team skills in order to be successful in most jobs. Team learning varies greatly. In some classes or labs, newer (or less experienced) students are paired with more experienced students to learn an assigned task. In others, students are put together in groups to solve problems or make decisions on a case. Some professors have their students do research as a team and present their findings in a formal presentation.

Marie McKendall at Grand Valley State University says that in order for team projects to be successful, students must see them as meaningful and relevant. She also stresses the importance of making students aware of the time commitment involved in learning to work as a team.[1] Explain to your students why you assign team projects and the goals you hope they achieve. Using teams in the classroom allows students to develop skills in leadership, communication, negotiation, and decision-making.

If you use teams in your classroom, you will need to decide how to assign students to teams, how to teach team skills, how to help teams with accountability, and how to deal with complaints about individual team members.

Assigning Teams

There are a number of ways to assign students to teams.

- Let students pick their own teammates. Keep in mind, though, that students tend to pick their friends and will not get the full experience of working with people who are different or unknown to them.

- Decide on the makeup of the team yourself. You could involve the students by having them write down several (you pick the number) people in the class they would like to have on their team as well as the names of persons with whom they do not want to work. Allocate some of the team members based on this information.

- Assign the students to teams based on some similar characteristic such as the same geographical living area to make it easier for the students to meet.

- Pick the team members with an eye for as much diversity on the teams as possible by choosing different majors, backgrounds, age groups, etc., on each team.

- Randomly assign students to teams by counting them off in class.

Try to make the team size fairly small. Consider limiting teams to four to five people although you will also have to consider the amount of class time it will take for the teams to make presentations. Some professors have teams videotape their presentations and then turn these in to be graded in order to save class time.

Team Building

A good way to help teams build cohesion is to do an exercise that allows the members to get to know each other. See box on next page for an example.

Also, consider using a team building exercise that illustrates that collectively students can make better decisions than they can individually. There are many paper and pencil exercises that either rank objects in terms of value or people in terms of life and death decisions. Some present students with scenarios such as surviving a plane crash in the ocean or in Northern Canada in winter. Others require the students to decide what you would need to survive if you were on the moon. Survival-type exercises are available at no cost on the Internet.[2] These exercises help the students realize that the potential for a better end product exists within their team and helps them to understand why they should want to work together.

The first exercise I have the teams do has nothing to do with the class subject matter. I tell them I want them to get to know each other better outside of class by doing something creative. They are to write up a one-page team paper describing what they did and how this allowed them to learn about each other. Photos of the activity are encouraged. I usually give them two weeks to do the activity and then they give a short presentation in class. I choose the team that is the most creative and recognize them (perhaps even giving a couple extra credit points). Past team activities have included writing a song about the class and singing it together; going to a pottery place and collaborating on painting a coffee mug; and making a memory bottle that was given to me to throw into the ocean the next trip I made to Florida (however, it was such a creative idea that I have kept the bottle in my office).

---Dr. Kirk

Tips for Managing Teams

Make sure the teams assign both task and group roles to each member. Each student should be formally responsible for specific tasks required to complete the project. Group roles would include duties such as scheduling meetings, keeping minutes, and typing up notes. Instruct the teams to require a "ticket" system where each team member must bring his or her completed task or research notes to every meeting. Have them keep track whether or not members brought their "ticket" for the day.

Set deadlines throughout the semester. For example, if the team is doing research, ask for their bibliography or an outline of the paper or presentation several weeks before the final project is due. Plan to meet with teams periodically to discuss their progress and any problems they have. Consider taking a few minutes once a week or so to meet with teams to see how they are doing and to answer questions.

> *I have my students do a 60 to 90 second overview of their team project to me. This is intended to simulate a person's opportunity to report on the progress of a project if they met their boss in an elevator. The students can have an index card with them with three talking points. They must be prepared to answer one or two quick questions from me. I do this around the middle of the semester to see how they are progressing.*
>
> **---Jon Beard**
> **Purdue University**

Peer Evaluations

The biggest complaint students have concerning team projects are teammates that do not do their share of the work. Using peer evaluations helps to hold each team member accountable for his or her own efforts. Ask for these at midterm when you can actually do something about any issues and again at the end of the semester to use in grading. The fact that you are collecting this information will keep most students honest.

Have each student fill out a self-evaluation form as well as a peer evaluation form for all other members of their team. See Figure 9.1 and 9.2 for sample forms. Explain that you expect them to take the evaluation seriously and that filling it out is part of their own participation grade. You should also encourage written comments.

Even if there are problems with their teammates, students tend to want to give all members of the team the same grade on peer evaluations. Explain that you do not expect everyone to get the same number of points. Using behaviorally anchored scales encourages students to evaluate on performance rather than personality.

Nancy Leonard at West Virginia University ties peer evaluations to the concept of bonuses. She instructs her students to evaluate their fellow teammates on the basis of time and effort spent and the quality of their work. Each team member gets a percentage of a hypothetical $200 bonus. See Figure 9.3 for an example of the form she uses.

In their book on *Classroom Assessment Techniques*, Angelo and Cross advocate using a group-work evaluation form that asks open-ended questions such as:[3]

- "Give one specific example of something the other group members learned from you that they probably wouldn't have learned otherwise?"

- "Suggest one change the group could make to improve its performance."

You might consider giving the teams the ability to "fire" a teammate for not doing their share of the work. If so, decide beforehand what the process will be to fire someone. That student would then have to do the project alone or take a zero for the project grade.

A way to involve the other students in the class is to have each team's classmates participate in grading the final presentations. Every person in class does a PCP (Praise, Critique, Polish) report on paper to turn in to you after the presentation:

- Praise: What did the team do well in their presentation?

- Critique: What could the team do to improve for their next presentation?

- Polish: What could the team have done to make the presentation look more professional?

Have each class member put their name on these evaluations and use it to determine that person's participation points for the day. These evaluations will also help you grade the teams as you will see the same comments mentioned over and over.

A Final Note

There are some real challenges to using teams in the classroom. Students tend not to like to work in teams, especially if their grade is tied to the ability and motivations of their teammates. It also take up class time if you require oral presentations by the teams. However, teams are used in most organizations today and learning how to work with others is a valuable lesson for your students.

> *I ask for progress reports at mid-term on my students' team projects. The report includes each team member's name, the team progress so far, each individual team member's responsibilities and tasks that they will be doing, and the due date of these tasks. At the end of the semester I give the teams a number of points and have them allocate these to all the members of the team based on how well they completed the tasks they were assigned.*
>
> **---Kay Ellen McGlashan**
> **Texas State University**

Figure 9.1: Sample Self Evaluation Form

Team # _____   Your Name _____

Using the scale of 5 = excellent team player to 1 = no help at all on project; evaluate your role in the team project.

1. Attendance at meetings?   5 4 3 2 1

2. Prepared for the meetings?   5 4 3 2 1

3. Contributed valuable ideas   5 4 3 2 1
   to the team?

4. Did your share of the work?   5 4 3 2 1

5. Took assignments seriously?   5 4 3 2 1

6. Prepared for your portion of   5 4 3 2 1
   the presentation?

7. Individual effort to finish   5 4 3 2 1
   written paper?

8. Open to others' ideas and   5 4 3 2 1
   suggestions?

9. Willingness to help other   5 4 3 2 1
   group members?

10. Overall, how would you rate   5 4 3 2 1
    yourself on this project?

Comments?

Figure 9.2: Sample Peer Evaluation Form for Teammates

Team#____Team Member's Name _____

Using the following scale of 5 = excellent team player to 1 = no help at all on project; evaluate each of your fellow team members.

1. Attendance at meetings?   5 4 3 2 1

2. Prepared for the meetings?   5 4 3 2 1

3. Contributed valuable ideas   5 4 3 2 1
   to the team?

4. Did their share of the work? 5 4 3 2 1

5. Took assignments seriously?   5 4 3 2 1

6. Prepared for their portion of 5 4 3 2 1
   the presentation?

7. Did individual effort to finish 5 4 3 2 1
   written paper?

8. Open to others' ideas and   5 4 3 2 1
   suggestions?

9. Willingness to help other   5 4 3 2 1
   group members?

10. Would you choose this per-   5 4 3 2 1
    son in the future?

Comments?

Figure 9.3: Peer Evaluation Form For Teams

Evaluate the relative contribution to the projects for each team member, including yourself. To do this, assume you have a bonus to divide among members. Feel free to divide the bonus as you feel appropriate - as long as the total adds up to $100 for time and effort and $100 for quality of work. This information will be used to evaluate individual efforts within teams. Your comments will be kept confidential.

Reward the amount of time and effort of each member on the teams assignments:

Name (yourself) _____	$_____
Group Member _____	$_____
Group Member _____	$_____
Group Member _____	$_____

TOTAL: $100.00

Reward the quality of work of each member on the assignments:

Name (yourself) _____	$_____
Group Member _____	$_____
Group Member _____	$_____
Group Member _____	$_____

TOTAL: $100.00

Source: Nancy Leonard, West Virginia University

Questions from Faculty

Dear Dr. Kirk:
My students complain that when they meet with their team members, the meetings are not very productive. How can I help them?
Hate Meetings Myself

Dear Hate Meetings,
This is a very real problem as it is estimated that half of the time spent in meetings in the work world is seen as ineffective and unproductive. Here are eight keys to effective meetings.

1. Decide if a meeting is really necessary or could the tasks be accomplished by e-mail, memo, or other methods of communication.
2. Have a distinct purpose and know what you want to accomplish at the meeting.
3. Have an agenda with a list of meeting goals that is distributed in advance.
4. Start on time and end on time (or sooner).
5. Maintain the focus at all times. If the meeting is over early, people can stick around to talk about other topics.
6. Capture action items that identify tasks to be done, by whom, and by what date.
7. Never hand out material at the beginning of a meeting as people will immediately start reading. If there is written material, send it out in advance of the meeting.
8. Send out minutes of the meeting within 24 hours that include "to-do" lists for all team members as well as the date for the next meeting.

Comments from Students

I had a great professor who brought in real world experience and examples. The semester project was meaningful and applied concepts learned from class. Instead of exams, there were weekly quizzes covering materials from previous classes. The course overall was challenging.

Andrew

I like professors that do activities, involve different types of media, and devote class periods to difficult case studies. It varies the routine and forces students to actively engage in learning and to attend class for participation points.

Sam

My best professors were great teachers because they motivated you to learn. Even though the subject might be dry and boring, they would find a way to motivate you to research it more and make it fun. If students enjoy what they are learning about, they are more likely to learn the material.

Nelson

In a philosophy class, I enjoyed my radical teacher. While I didn't agree with all he had to say, I had a lot of respect for his genuine interest in teaching students how to think for themselves and how to challenge conventional wisdom through analytical thought. He never voiced his actual opinion, but rather made us voice and challenge each other's viewpoints.

Patrick

Endnotes:

[1]McKendall, M., "Teaching Groups to Become Teams," *Journal of Education for Business*, May/June 2000, 75 (5), pp. 277-282.

[2]Free survival type exercises can be found at: www.wilderdom.com/games/descriptions/SurvivalScenarios.html

[3]Angelo, Thomas A. and K. Patricia Cross, *Classroom Assessment Techniques*, 2nd Edition, Jossey-Bass Publishers, 1993.

CHAPTER 10

Managing Large Classes

*A teacher who is attempting to teach
without inspiring the pupil with a desire
to learn is hammering on a cold iron.*
---Horace Mann

Some of you may be thinking to yourselves that it sounds great to talk about making a connection with your students, taking attendance, requiring participation, and so forth, but how do you do so in a large class? How do you make students want to come to class and learn when they feel that they are just mere faces in the crowd? The following are suggestions on how to deal with issues that occur in all classroom settings but seem to be more problematic in larger classes.

Attendance and Tardiness

Since students feel anonymous in large classes, taking attendance is a good way of encouraging them to come to class. Give points for attendance or tell your students that you will use attendance in cases where their grade is borderline. Another way to encourage students to attend class is to give bonus points for perfect attendance. There are a number of methods to track attendance such as having a sign-up sheet at the door, taking up homework, or using a seating chart.

I teach classes of 200 to 225 students. Attendance counts as 10% of their grade, which some of the students gripe about, but studies have shown that attendance is a good predictor of grades. It's my contention that it is important to attend class and I want the grade percentage to be large enough that it can actually make a significant difference in the students' final grade calculation. I usually take attendance at the beginning of the class period by passing around a preprinted attendance roster with everyone's name on it; they have to sign their name and put down the last four numbers of their student ID. If I notice a big difference in the number of empty chairs before or after break, I'll pass around the roster again...they usually quit playing that game after the first week. I allow the students two unexcused absences before their attendance grade is affected, with a sliding scale based on the number of absences they have at the end of the quarter. I also use individual self-assessment exercises as 15% of their grade. They have to be in the class to turn those in. Missing a few of the exercises can damage their grade significantly, but they can also help if the students do not test well.

---C. Aaron Kelley
Ohio University

Start each class period on time so students realize that they will miss important information if they are tardy. On the first day of class, tell your students that you expect them to arrive and be seated on time so that they do not interrupt the lecture. Also, tell them that if they do happen to be tardy, they should sit down quietly close to the door. Ask them to see you or your teaching assistant after class to get credit for attendance. You can use that opportunity to remind them of the attendance policy.

At the beginning of each class, consider reviewing the lecture notes from the previous class. Point out potential exam questions. You might also give random pop quizzes during the first few minutes of class that cannot be made up to encourage students to come on time.

Motivating Students
Students in large classes, just as those in smaller ones, will "buy into" the class if the students find the topics interesting and they think they can apply the major points to their future careers or lives. Having a motivator such as points for attendance and participation does not hurt either. Try some or all of the following to motivate your students.

If possible, move around the classroom to keep the students' attention. Tell stories based on your own work experiences to personalize the lecture. Present information that is not in the book but which will be on their exams. Exam questions could also come from information provided by guest speakers or questions and examples from the students themselves.

Put the students into small groups for activities done both in or outside of class. This allows the students to meet a few of their classmates which will make them feel more comfortable. It also gives them someone to contact in the event they miss a class and need the lecture notes. Give credit for these group activities although you do not need to grade them. The students must attend class to get these points.

> *Although I complained about it, professors that don't put their lecture notes online force us to go to class. Lectures had to be interesting, fun, or out of the ordinary, even if it was only once in a while. I had to have a good reason to make myself go and sit still for an hour, knowing that no one would notice if I wasn't there. If I feel some sort of a personal connection with a professor, I feel much more obligated to go. I guess the biggest difference was that I had some professors that forced us to go to lectures, and great professors that made me <u>want</u> to go to lectures.*
> ---**Tricia Joseph, 2005 graduate**
> **University of Iowa**

Getting Participation

One complaint of large classes is that the students tend to be passive and detached. The best way to get them involved is to learn as many students' names as possible. Try to arrive at the classroom early and stay after class to engage the students in small talk. Stand at the door, give out your handouts, and greet as many students as you can by name. At the very least, say hello. Consider requiring your students to wear name tags with their first name in very large letters. If students raise their hands with a question, ask for their names and use them when answering.

Many professors claim that they are not very good at remembering names. However, a lot of high school teachers have large classes and will not only know all of their students' names, they will know additional information about each student such as the school activities they participate in. Consider taking photos of the students (with their permission) during the first week of class. Write each student's name on the back of his or her photo and flip through these several times a day to match names to faces. You might put the photos in order of the seating chart and learn their names by where they sit in class. The students will be impressed by your effort to get to know them; you will also have fewer behavioral issues if they think that you can identify who they are.

> *A joke going around college campuses involves a student who arrives late to an exam in his class of 300 students. He works feverishly until well after the examination time is over. As he goes to turn in the exam, the professor states that he cannot accept the exam as it is late. The student protests loudly, stating, "Do you KNOW who I AM?" The professor, bewildered, says, "No..." The student smiles, quickly slips the exam into the middle of the stack, and leaves.*
> **---Anonymous Student**

If you give out your lecture notes, leave blanks so that the students have to follow the lecture to fill in the missing information. Put questions in your lecture outlines that the students will be asked to answer. This also reminds you to stop and give the students time to answer those questions.

Be enthusiastic about the subject matter and bring in as many current examples as possible. Ask the students to bring in journals, newspaper articles, or web site entries they find relevant to the class to get participation points. You might ask the students to give a 15 second presentation to the class on the material they brought in.

Post your office hours on the board each day. and encourage students to come see you. Require those students who are doing poorly in class to sign up for an appointment with you.

Examinations

You will want to make your grading objectives especially clear if you are using teaching assistants to help grade. Use multiple-choice exams or develop a rubric for short answer or essay questions. Avoid makeup exams by giving several exams or quizzes and allowing the students to drop their lowest score. If they miss an exam or quiz, that would be the one they would drop. This motivates students to take all the exams and quizzes on time so the decision is theirs as to which grade is dropped. Chapter 8 on Managing Exams also provides some suggestions on giving exams in large classes.

Obtaining Feedback

In a small class, you can usually tell by facial expressions and body language if the students do not understand the material. However, this is more difficult to do in a large class. Stop every 10 to 15 minutes and pick a row of students and tell them that you want someone in that row to ask you a question. Or, use Dave Bloomquist's suggestion from Chapter 2. Professor Bloomquist uses a Testometer to judge how difficult to make his tests. This is based on whether or not the students ask questions. The more questions the students ask, the easier the test because he tells them the material must thus be difficult.

In the article, *"Beating the Numbers Game: Effective Teaching in Large Classes,"* Richard Felder advocates using an in-class exercise to get the students involved.[1] He stops on a periodic basis during lecture and assigns a task to the students. They have a limited time to complete the assignment. He then calls on various students to answer, picking those in the back of the room disproportionately. He uses these exercises because they get the students participating as they think they might be called on. In addition, the act of doing something, rather than just listening, helps the students learn.

In their book, *Classroom Assessment Techniques*, Angelo and Cross advocate doing a one-minute paper at the end of each class.[2] Students are asked to answer some variation of the following two questions. You can then read these and answer them orally at the next class session.

- What was the most important thing you learned today in class?

- What important question regarding the class material do you still have?

Another method of getting feedback is to form a student committee made up of volunteers from the class. These students would meet with you every two to three weeks and provide feedback on assignments, exams, lectures, and classroom management. It is not necessary to give extra credit to these students. Students appreciate being asked to give input as well as getting to know you on a more personal basis.

Ending the Class

One problem that is prevalent in any class but is especially noticeable in large classes is students packing up to leave a few minutes before the class actually ends. The noise level can be disruptive to both the professor and the other students. To reduce this problem, consider using the last few minutes of class to assign homework problems that will be taken up at the next meeting. You could use these assignments as a form of attendance. Or, you could try giving the students a sample test question at the end of class. Another method is to provide a dismissal cue by putting up a cartoon or other visual at the official end of your lecture. Students will get used to waiting for that cue. Promise the students that you will end the class on time so that they can get to their other commitments and be sure that you do so.

A Final Note

Teaching a large class is similar in many respects to teaching a smaller one. You need to get and keep the students' attention. This can be done by using a variety of presentation methods, including lecture, guest speakers, videos, overheads or Power Point, and group activities. Make the class relevant to the students so they will want to come to class. Tell stories and use humor when appropriate. Move around the room as much as possible so that the students have to follow you with their eyes. Repeat a student's question so that everyone can hear it before you answer. Reward for attendance in some way. Treat your students with respect and try to get to know as many of them as possible on a more personal basis. Deal with disruptive students as soon as the inappropriate behavior occurs. Figure 10.1 contains some additional tips from a former computer engineering student on managing a large classroom.

I heard about a professor of a large class of 200+ students who has a policy that the first time a cell phone rings during class, it is considered a warning. The next time a phone rings, all of the students are given a pop quiz. Let's just say the students are very diligent about turning off their cell phones in his class.

---Dr. Kirk

Figure 10.1: Tips From a Former Student

- Be animated. Lecture halls are huge and for the people in the back, you make-up 1% of their field of vision. Move a LOT. Use massive arm motions, jump up and down, have wild hand gestures. Seriously, students are like reptiles, our vision is based on motion.

- Tell stories and jokes. Find ways to make boring theories come to life. If your subject material can't make for a fun story that captures peoples' attention, why are you teaching it? Virtually anything can be made interesting to the people who need to learn it.

- Don't allow students to be passive. You can't really get any one-on-one feedback from a student in a 200-person lecture hall. What you CAN do is make them fear not paying attention. Throw paper airplanes. Find excuses to walk around the room. Do demonstrations. The point is to keep your students on their toes.

- Develop a class community, both in and out of class. In class, have everyone do zany stupid things if that's what it takes. Have everyone stand up, then have the left-handed people move to the left of the class and the right-handed to the right (or whatever fits the lecture you're giving). Keep the students moving periodically to help them stay focused and wide-awake. Out of

Figure 10.1 continued

class, set up forums, or bulk "question and answer hours" where you or a TA will be around if students need questions answered.

- Focus on group projects. This allows for more challenging and involved homework projects and allows you to consolidate students into smaller student groups. Students will check with their groups before bothering you for an answer, you'll have less work to grade, and collaboration tends to lead to better understanding. Sure, there are some who will slack off and not participate but usually groups will tell you which of their teammates is dead weight.

Source: Christopher T. Kirk,
2003 graduate of Iowa State University

Questions from Faculty

Dear Dr. Kirk:
Are students more likely to misbehave in larger classes than small ones?

Lecture Hall Prof

Dear Lecture Hall Prof,
Students may perceive that it is easier to get away with disruptive behavior in larger classes. However, that "perception" can be manipulated by you. Let the students know you are paying attention, try to learn their names, and correct disruptive behavior the day it occurs. Even in large classes students will be more likely to respect the class rules if they respect you.

Dear Dr. Kirk:
How do you cope with those "putting away noises" that occur when you still have five minutes left of the class? It is a real problem in a large class.

But I'm Not Done Yet

Dear Not Done,
Address the issue the first day and again whenever you hear students packing up early. Consider taking attendance or giving a quiz at the end of the class. Or, tell the students that you will give them one potential test question at the end of each day's lecture so that they will wait for it. Don't make the statement that you are running out of time as that will be a cue for students to leave. Instead, remind them that you still have five minutes left and continue your lecture.

Comments from Students

I never went to class and still got an "A," it wasn't challenging, the teacher didn't even know who I was, and I saw the class as a waste of time.

Jill

I had professors who demanded attendance in large classes, and enforced it with (seriously!) attendance slips. Students would rotate attendance, carrying the attendance slips for the group...slightly more irritating but equally effective is the student who would show up, drop off the attendance slip, and then leave the class.

Chris

My geoscience professor (my last semester of school, night class, met only once a week...really tough to get me to go) would bring in pictures and things for his Power Point from his own trips, his family, things like that. If I feel some sort of a personal connection with a professor, I feel much more obligated to attend class. Otherwise, I felt anonymous in these large classes.

Tricia

If a professor simply reads off the usual old lecture slides without adding much and makes the slides available on the web, I didn't attend class. If you're really a listen-to-a-lecture type learner, you read the slides before class and determine if you need to learn that day. (Hey, maybe I'm abnormal but there were plenty of days where there just wasn't anything for me to learn!)

Christopher

Endnotes:

[1]Felder, Richard, "Beating the Numbers Game: Effective Teaching in Large Classes," paper presented at the 1997 ASEE Annual Conference, Milwaukee, WI. (found at www.ncsu.edu/felder-public/Papers/Largeclasses.htm)

[2]Angelo, Thomas and K. Patricia Cross, *Classroom Assessment Techniques: A Handbook for College Teachers*, 2nd edition, Jossey-Bass, 1993.

CHAPTER 11

Managing Online Classes

prof, i luv this www class, im sittin in my pjs right now workin on the stuff 4 class, but im fraid this assgnmt is gun b late. cud u gimme n x10shun til fri? srry. wont hppen again. ttyl
---Anonymous Web Student

Computers and the Internet have given professors the ability to move beyond the traditional brick and mortar classroom setting to one where students can be engaged in learning 24 hours a day. In 2002, over 3.1 million students enrolled in courses that were conducted completely online.[1] In addition, traditional lecture classes are moving towards using the web to facilitate learning. This trend means that students must adapt to using online technologies to do research assignments. According to one recent study, "49 percent of college students first began to use the Internet (for research purposes) when they entered college."

This chapter was written by Dr. Bradley Meyer, Drake University. Dr. Meyer has been teaching online classes since 1996.

This change in pedagogy means many of the skills professors have learned in managing the classroom are now useless in this cyberspace environment. However, online classes are not necessarily more difficult to manage than a traditional class, they are just different.

> *In 1996, I taught my first Internet class. Twenty-two faceless students and I interacted online for seven weeks. I had used computer technology quite extensively before this web class, but now the computer became my sole pedagogical context. However, I can honestly say that once I accepted that I would have to change how I managed the class, teaching online was a delightful experience.*
>
> **---Dr. Meyer**

How is Teaching Online Different?

Are you an expert in reading the body language of your students in order to determine if they are engaged and understanding your lectures? Until bandwidth greatly increases, web communication in online classes will primarily be textual so you will no longer be able to use this visual cue. You can videotape your lectures and make streaming video files that your students can watch, but any discussion will take place through the keyboard. In addition, you will find proofreading every message you send to your students to be very time consuming. You will also see that students do not mind sending messages to you or their classmates with misspellings. On the contrary, they often misspell purposefully, in order to cut letters out of a word. They have their own language consisting of emoticons, abbreviated words, character substitutions, and a lack of traditional punctuation. It's part of the online culture.

Are you good at managing a discussion, thinking quickly on your feet, and drawing out points by taking the class step by step through a logical argument in fine Socratic fashion? Most computer software that facilitates class discussions will post comments one by one in a hierarchical list. You, or other students in the class, can make a response to anyone else's comments. This kind of discussion does not remain linear as in a classroom where only one person can speak at a time. Rather, it grows like a tree; branches sprout in many directions as some students reply to existing posts and others begin new trains of thought. In addition, any online 'discussion' will stretch out over several days with time lags between posts. This calls for management skills different from those used in the classroom.

Perhaps you have developed a set of techniques to prevent cheating on exams similar to those discussed earlier in Chapter 8. Ensuring integrity in exams and assignments completed online requires a different strategy. Students who are allowed to choose their own exam locations will have access to telephone, e-mail, and Internet chat. They may even have relatives or friends serving as consultants, sitting in the same room while they are taking the exam.

Online classes are still new enough that most students, as well as professors, do not really know what to expect. Thus, setting up your expectations and communicating them is extremely important. This chapter will cover issues of setting class expectations, connecting with your students, encouraging participation, managing online exams, and managing your time.

Setting Class Expectations

Setting expectations for your online class is just as critical as for a traditional course. In each new class you will probably get several e-mails from students who will inform you that they have never taken a web class before. They will ask a lot of questions and display a perceivable lack of confidence in class procedures. It also takes some students a little time to realize that the professor is a real person and is subject to a finite commitment of time to the course. They are used to interacting with web sites that are open 24 hours a day. Their subconscious mental picture is that you are always sitting at your computer, ready to answer their questions and reply to their posts.

Chapters 3 and 4 discussed managing your students' impressions and the first day of class. While you may not have a typical 'first day of class,' you will at least have a first point of contact. The first point of contact will usually be the web site for the class.

> *I recommend that you initiate contact before class even begins by sending out an email message to your students. You can introduce yourself and explain how the course will work. Such an email also signals to the students that you are organized and concerned about their getting off to a good start in the class.*
>
> **---Dr. Meyer**

You need to provide your students with a clear explanation of the class and a set of expectations. This could be a section in a syllabus, but because the protocols for an online class are so different from a traditional course, you may want a separate document explaining how your class will be conducted. This document should explain your class policies and procedures that are unique to online education including:

- How you will communicate with the students and how they will communicate with you;
- How the timing and due dates of assignments will be implemented and enforced;
- How you expect the students to interact with other classmates and how often;
- Whether you require work to be done independently or whether they are allowed to collaborate on assignments;
- When you will be online and available to answer questions;
- How exams will be conducted (if the class includes exams);
- What they should do and whom they should contact if they encounter computer problems;

- what specialized tools will be required for the course;
- any computer system requirements on operating system, browser, or internet connection.

This document could be sent to students before class starts as an e-mail message. Also, post it on the class web site. You might try writing up your procedures in a FAQ (frequently asked questions) format. Since you are communicating this in writing rather than orally, you will have to take extra effort to communicate your spirit as well as your content.

Connecting With Your Students

Because of the impersonal nature of web communication, you will need to take special initiative to connect personally with the students. For example, your picture should be posted on the web site where your class materials are. To take it one step farther, add the sound of your voice. It is a fairly simple matter to record a 30 second introduction to a topic and digitize it for delivery over the web. Thirty seconds is not time to say much, but if the students hear your voice, you become more real to them.

Some professors require their students to send in or post pictures of themselves so that no one in the class remains faceless. However, some students will be hesitant to have their picture online. There are both privacy and security concerns. If you post class pictures, make sure you do so on a password protected page. This way only the members of the class have access to the pictures and they won't show up on a Google image search. Remember, there is no guarantee that the students will send you an actual picture of themselves, so do not be surprised if you have several members of the class who look just like Justin Timberlake or Jennifer Lopez.

> *When I return assignments, I try to add a few words that expresses my personal interest in the student—it's like eye contact and a smile.*
> ---**Dr. Meyer**

Using Forums to Get Student Participation

If you are used to teaching in a classroom and are fairly new to the web, you might wonder if it is truly possible to create a classroom discussion without face-to-face interaction. For the current generation of college students, it is much easier than you might imagine. Kids who have grown up with access to Internet are accustomed to interacting via chat rooms, forums, text messaging, and e-mail. The days of the teenager tying up the phone have given way to the teenager tying up the computer. It is not at all uncommon for a student to be interacting with five chat windows, two web sites, and three applications simultaneously. Your biggest challenge with requiring online discussions may be your own lack of experience with monitoring several conversation threads at the same time.

As an educator, you are trying to facilitate student participation in the course topics. Web forums allow discussions to be used in online classes and can be an excellent way for students to interact and develop relationships with you and each other. You, as the professor, could post a question or topic and the students would be able to respond to it and to each other's responses over a period of time. However, there are some unique aspects to managing an online forum that are different from managing a traditional classroom discussion. These include issues regarding the quantity and quality of posts as well as breaking down larger classes into manageable sizes for discussion purposes.

<u>Quantity of Posts</u>
One problem you will have is that some students will not post anything until the last minute and others seem to be on the computer all the time posting thoughts and replies. Discussions in traditional classrooms have these same issues. You can try using the techniques for handling the Shy Student or the Class Hog that are discussed in Chapter 7. However, online classes pose some unique problems in managing these types of students.

You can try posing a question in the forum specifically to a student who is not participating, but if the student doesn't get online and read the forum until the last minute, this may not work. A better approach may be to pose the question in an e-mail. Students check e-mail more often than they check forums. In addition, students will not feel embarrassed by a comment sent via e-mail. However, they might be embarrassed by one posted for the entire class to see.

Students who dominate the online discussion may need some boundaries, such as a maximum number of posts allowed. An e-mail message with a gentle reminder to avoid hogging the conversation might be appropriate. You may find it useful to engage an especially talkative (but knowledgeable) student in a conversation outside of the discussion forum.

You can manage the online discussion by setting posting requirements. For example, tell the students to make at least one post in response to another student's post. Set up specific response deadlines, such as having the first post due by Tuesday at 6:00 p.m. The second post, which is a response to the first, would then be due within 48 hours. If you are trying to encourage participation, a good required posting frequency would be one post every two to three days. This is a reasonable compromise between student availability and necessary discussion to make the exchange cooperative and meaningful.

Quality of Posts

Realize that you will have less give and take in your online forums. On average, each student's post will tend to be more thoughtful than a random statement made in a class, but the time lag between replies does not allow for a large number of point-counterpoint responses. Do not be frustrated if it seems like you do not really finish forum conversations. You may have to settle for providing a summary yourself, or asking a student to do so and move on to the next topic.

Provide direction for the responsive posts such as, "You must point out one thing you agree with about the other student's post and one thing you disagree with or feel is incomplete." Ask students to provide support for their statements. Add your own comments into the forum to stimulate discussion. Avoid saying, "John is correct here and the rest of you missed the point." Instead, say, "What do you think about John's point? Is his line of reasoning correct or not?" You may want to develop a rubric for evaluating posts and provide this to the students. See Figure 11.1 for an example.

Some students are hesitant to type what they really think, especially on controversial subjects. Your forum software will allow for anonymous posts. Or, you could allow your students to use a screen name for that class. You would know the students' screen name, but their fellow classmates would not. If you use this option, then you may get more honest comments (including some offensive comments—the trade-off.) The best option, however, is to create an environment where differences of opinion are welcome and everyone is treated with respect.

Assigning Groups
Consider breaking up the class into smaller groups of students. Create individual forums for each group. The students will not get to know the entire class, but they will interact with a smaller circle of people and be able to participate more often. This subdivision also simplifies managing the discussions.

Managing Online Exams

There are several ways to conduct exams for online classes. Many professors implement what would be the classical take-home exam, meaning that students can download the exam, work on it at their leisure, and send it back by a due date.

Another approach is to allow the student to decide when the exam will be taken, but to enforce a time limit for the exam. You can manage exam time limits with a course management system like Blackboard or Web CT. For example, the student might be given 30 minutes to answer a set of multiple-choice questions. The software enforces the time limit for each student whenever they choose to take the exam. You may want to have a policy stating that you do not answer questions during the exam. For example, you may have one student taking an exam who e-mails you with a question that you are able to clarify because you were online during their exam time. A second student might have the same question but not be able to reach you during the limited time frame.

An alternative approach to this issue would be to set up a small number of fixed exam times. Students can take the exam during any one of the chosen time periods and you guarantee that you will be available via e-mail to address questions.

> *I use three set time periods for each exam. Usually I pick a Friday evening, a Saturday late afternoon and a Sunday early afternoon. I determine a fixed two-hour block of time on those days and require the students to send me an email one week before the exam and tell me the exam period they choose. I set up the exam in Blackboard with password protection and send the password to the students just before their two-hour block is to begin. There is usually a student or two who are unable to take the exam in any of the three time periods. I then set up an individual time period for these students. This method reduces the number of exam times, so I can make myself available for questions during those times.*
>
> **---Dr. Meyer**

Maintaining Integrity

Chapters 7 and 8 discuss how to handle students who cheat. However, online classes offer a greater challenge to ensure integrity. Without your personal presence, students can more easily bend the rules. Some students will turn in their work late, have outside help during exams, and turn in reports with text they have borrowed heavily from un-cited sources. The lack of a physical classroom seems to encourage ethical risk taking. Even something as simple as a time limit can be abused. You may have had a student who continues working on the exam until after the end of the class period in a traditional class. You announce that it is time to collect the exam, but the student does not budge. Out of the kindness of your heart, you give him or her another few minutes. Finally, you stand up to walk out the door and the student runs the test to you just as you leave. Students taking online exams will miss your deadlines also and will then have excuses as to why it took so long to take the test. You are then faced with the decision of how to penalize the student. It is best to stick with your stated policy, but if you are softhearted, that may be more easily said than done. It can be a tough balancing act to make allowance for legitimate excuses without allowing students to be rewarded for dishonesty.

From: Online Class Student
To: Dr. Meyer
Subject: Why my exam was late

- They were rewiring the Internet connection in my fraternity house so I had to wait until they were done to send in my exam.
- My cat got tangled up in the power cord and unplugged my computer and I lost all my work.
- My monitor went out right in the middle of the exam. I had to go to the store to buy a new one.
- It was storming and my power went out. I had to go to my friend's house to finish the exam.
- My child started throwing up and I had to help him.
- Construction workers severed the phone line outside my house.

Perhaps in the long run the only way to insure integrity will be to require students to take exams in person at a testing center, with photo identification. Until then, it is important to be on the lookout for cheating and to find ways to make cheating more work than learning the material.

The first time I taught my web class, I was highly suspicious that students might cooperate on exams. The class was a mathematical course and I told the students that it was acceptable for them to work together on problems as long as each person was contributing and learning. I made note throughout the class as to which students turned in assignments that looked similar and appeared in my email at about the same time. I made sure that those people who appeared to be working together got different versions of the exam. I tried to make it as difficult as possible for the students to cheat. My plan seemed to work. I didn't find signs of cooperation on the exams...or so I thought. Early the next semester I ran into one of the students from the class. She mentioned that several students from the class were sitting together in a computer lab during the exam and conferred with each other on the questions. Needless to say, I was quite irked.

---Dr.Meyer

Managing Time Demands

Teaching an online course is time consuming, especially the first couple times you teach the class. Allow yourself plenty of preparation time to get ready for the class and then anticipate that it will take more time that you had expected while class is in session.

To help you manage your time, remember that you do not have to write a comment in response to every post. In some cases, you can add a summary post after a set of student posts and just refer to the entire discussion. Students will know that you have read all the posts and thought about them. Keep in mind that students find it discouraging to get no feedback whatsoever.

> *My advice to colleagues teaching online courses would be time management, specifically in terms of establishing guidelines on e-mails and voice mails. I would have students contact me at literally all hours of the day and night. In Paloff's, "Building Learning Communities in Cyberspace," he states that where an instructor might spend 2.5 hours per week in a live class, one could easily spend 2.5 hours per DAY responding to e-mails and posts in an online course. In my next class, I plan to have some type of established timeframe each day/week that students can know I will be responding to messages.*
>
> **---Johnna Neary**
> **Drake University**

Develop rubrics to grade assignments, forum posts, and exams. You may want to create a file of comments that you can cut and paste into your feedback. You do not have to assign a grade to every single post. For some assignments you can simply give a pass/no pass grade.

Have students post questions on assignments in the forum rather than e-mailing them to you. When you respond to a question, both the question and your response will be available to everyone in the class, not just the student who initiated the question. You can also allow other students to answer the questions posed as part of their class participation.

A Final Note

While physical classrooms will always exist, there will be a higher percentage of educational experiences occurring online in the future. The first time you teach an Internet class, prepare yourself for an adventure and realize that most of the issues you face in the classroom have their counterparts in cyberspace. Students will still have reasons as to why they could not do what you wanted them to do. Professor Jim Dodd shares a list of excuses he has encountered while teaching online accounting courses in Figure 11.2.

Many of the skills discussed in this book on setting your expectations and communicating these to your students are the same. While you will have to rely much more heavily on the written word, and you won't get to look your students in the eye, you can still develop a connection with your students, and that's what teaching is all about.

> *Don't feel intimidated by your 18 to 20-year-old students. They are point-click individuals and will not read instructions. Not all of them are as technology savvy as we older faculty tend to think.*
>
> **---Jim Dodd**
> **Drake University**

Figure 11.1: Sample Rubric for Forum Posts

Timeliness

5 points	Posted on time, 200-250 words; replied to minimum of 2 others.
4 points	Posted on time; less than 200 words;
3 points	Posted 1-2 days late; less than 200 words;
0-2 pts	Posted over 2 days late; less than 200 words; no replies

Content

5 points	Thoughtful and insightful; subject given appropriate depth.
4 points	Somewhat thoughtful; subject given appropriate depth.
3 points	Discussed at surface level; needs more depth.
0-2 pts	Confused, hard to follow

Context

5 points	Few stylistic errors; organized; clear communication.
4 points	Few stylistic errors; not always organized; direct & fairly clear communication.
3 points	Stylistic errors; organization weak; not always direct & clear communication.
0-2 pts	Stylistic errors; organization weak; no communication.

Figure 11.2: Tips for Students in How to Perform Poorly in an Online Course

1. Do not bother to order your text until week three. After you flunk several quizzes, tell your professor that the course is harder than you thought it would be. Ask to re-take the first five quizzes as you were not able to do any of the homework problems from the text.

2. Have your brother or sister take the course for you and brag about your fraud while drinking in a bar. Don't look around to see if there are others from the university that might report your behavior back to the professor.

3. Do not participate in Chapter Discussion Forums. Discussion Forum participation points can, at most, only affect your course grade one or two letter grades. When you discover <u>after</u> the cut-off date that points are actually assigned for participation, tell your professor that you could not find the chapter discussion forum so you should not be penalized for not participating.

4. Ignore the "time windows" for taking chapter quizzes and for making postings to the Discussion Forums. They obviously apply to everyone but you.

5. Do not work the homework; the homework solutions are already provided, so just scan them before taking the quiz.

6. Invest no more than 8-10 hours per week studying even though the teacher suggests

a <u>minimum</u> of 30-40 hours weekly.

7. Go backpacking for a month through small towns in Greece where there is sometimes no electricity even though this means you will not have Internet access for your class. Ask your professor if you can earn extra points for this lack, perhaps a paper on the life and culture that you observed while on your vacation. Ask to have this "extra paper" replace your low or missing scores on your accounting quizzes.

8. Enroll in an online course and then embark on a trip to Europe; do not bother to check your e-mail while out of the country. When you return two weeks into the course, tell your professor that the cities you visited (Paris, Rome, London) did not have Internet access so you were unable to log on. Convey immediate surprise that the course would start without you.

9. Work a full-time job, take two other summer courses concurrently with the online course, and ask yourself why this class is so demanding. Given your busy summer and conflicting priorities, have your spouse, sibling, or parent contact your professor to explain why the online class is at the bottom of your priority list. Ask the professor to give you a grading scale that is different than that of the rest of the students in the online class.

Source: Actual examples from prior online accounting classes taught by Jim Dodd, Drake University.

Questions from Faculty

Dear Dr. Meyer:

Do you have a recommendation about course management software? I have one friend who swears by Blackboard, another who loves Web CT and still another who prefers to set up his own pages using Frontpage. What do you suggest?

Ready to Start

Dear Ready to Start,

There are several choices for putting up a course web site.

- The do-it-yourself approach. I wouldn't do this unless you are a techie and have lots of time. This method of attack has the advantage that you can set up everything exactly how you like it, with no restrictions, but requires more knowledge and digital finesse that most of us have.

- Outsource the work. This will require that you explain the course structure and provide content to a web expert, either at your school or an outside company, and the web work is done for you. This is a great solution for those who have the resources, which many universities do not. An example of such a company is eCollege, but there are others.

- Use a course development package such as Blackboard or Web CT. This is the solution of choice for most professors at this time. The features in these packages continue to evolve and improve. However, for the best support, such software should be implemented at the college or university level. This ultimately means that for most of us, the decision is made for us by our school.

- Use the textbook company's web site. More and more textbooks come with support web sites that contain many of the features of the course management software, with content already built in. This reduces the administrative burden, and certainly is an approach to consider if you can find a text you like that has such a companion web site.

Dear Dr. Meyer:
I have just been told by my department chair that I am going to teach a web course next semester. I teach poetry and am used to in-class poetry readings and critique by the class. Can I make this work online?

Apprehensive

Dear Apprehensive,
Yes, you can make it work. In fact, the professor who led the charge to put courses online at my school ten years ago taught poetry. Discussion forums will work well for you, but I recommend that you require your students to buy an inexpensive microphone for their computer and create audio files of their poetry. The files can be made available online as an attachment to a discussion post and the students can listen and comment just like you have been doing for years. You'll have to decide on a standard audio format

for the files and tell the students what software to use. Hopefully, you have a tech support person who can help you make those decisions. I think you'll find the students will love it.

Dear Dr. Meyer:
What do I do about two students who are turning in duplicate assignments? How do I know who is doing the work and who is mooching?
Disturbed

Dear Disturbed,
I guess it all depends on the ground rules you have set. If you told the class that working together was not permissible, you can implement the appropriate consequences. If you told the class that they can work together, you might have to simply trust that both students are contributing to the effort. There is no sure way to find out who is doing what. It might be that your tests will reveal if one is learning and one is not. But that is only if you can give them different exams that they have to take at the same time with a time limit that makes it nearly impossible for one person to do both exams.

I have developed an exam template in Excel with numerical values throughout that are generated randomly using the student's ID number as the random number generator seed. Thus, no two exams are alike. This prevents copying of exam answers and makes it more difficult for two members of the class to help each other on an exam. Even after inventing these customized exams, another instance of cooperative exam taking came to my attention. I gave an exam one summer that was mostly quantitative, but with one problem that had some interpretation of results. Two students, who I had already deduced were friends, had wording that was very similar on these questions. In addition, they both made the same conceptual mistake on one of the other questions. I did a little exploratory work and found that the two exams were emailed from the same IP address. I also found that they were both last saved on the same computer. I e-mailed the students and told them that their exams looked suspicious to me and asked if they had interacted at all during the exam. They were emphatic that they had worked independently. Ultimately, I made them each take the exam over, in person. On a similar vein, last summer I heard from a colleague about a student of his who was offered several hundred dollars to take a class for someone else. We are only kidding ourselves if we think such things are not happening.

Comments from Students

The bad thing about on-line classes is not having good examples or not knowing what is expected. Another problem is professors not e-mailing you back in a timely matter.

Melissa

I think web courses have their pros and cons. I took 3 web-based classes simultaneously this summer and it was not the best decision I ever made. They are very time consuming and require more reading than a normal class would. On the flip side, web courses do give you the flexibility to finish your work on your own time. You definitely need to have excellent time management skills in order to succeed in web courses.

Sajani

I think that a good web instructor shows interest in the students' education by encouraging them to ask questions and by responding promptly. I also think that it is necessary to state the requirements of the course early on in the semester so that everyone knows how the course will be graded.

Jenelle

I had to take finance online and that was a great experience in part because of my professor. He assigned work and the day after it was due, he would always send us the solutions with the problems worked out. That helped me greatly.

Patricia

Endnotes:

[1]Thomas, D. "Distance Education Continues Apace at Postsecondary Institutions." www.ed.gov/news/pressreleases/2003/07/07182003.html

[2]Jones, S. "The Internet Goes to College: How Students are Living in the Future With Today's Technology." www.pewinternet.org/reports/pdfs/PIP_College_Report.pdf

CHAPTER 12

On Becoming a More Effective Teacher

*Good teachers are glad when a term
begins and a little sad when it ends.*
                              ---Margaret Mead

There is a typical life cycle for college professors. If you are new to teaching, the first few years are the survival years. During this time, you will be mostly concerned with not embarrassing yourself in front of your students. Educators at this stage tend to take one of two approaches: they are either very strict so the students do not see how unsure and nervous they are or they are casual and informal, wanting their students to like them. Eventually, you will become more comfortable and develop a style of teaching that fits your personality. After several more years of teaching, you will arrive at a stage where you need to develop new approaches to stay interested and to prevent burnout. High on the list is having a classroom where there is mutual respect and you can feel you are contributing to your students' future success.

This chapter presents some suggestions to help you become a more effective teacher.

Develop Your Own Philosophy of Teaching

According to Matt Kaplan at the University of Michigan, all professors have a teaching philosophy even if they have not written this down formally. He states that as a student for many years and now as an instructor, you have ideas and opinions about what works in the classroom.[1] The trick is to get on paper what you believe about teaching and learning and how this is reflected in your teaching methods.

Think about what it is you are trying to do in the classroom. Are you passing on a body of knowledge of a specific subject to the students? Are you teaching them how to learn? Are you giving them practical information on how to be an expert in their field of study? Are you role-modeling skills to help students become productive, useful members of society? Or, perhaps you aim to do all of the above? The readings, assignments, and exams you choose to give your students should reflect what you are trying to accomplish. Figure 12.1 presents an example of a teaching philosophy.

> *When I first interviewed at Drake University, I met with a group of students who asked me what my philosophy of teaching was. It was the first time I had even thought of that question. And while I managed to stammer out an acceptable answer, I realized that I needed to take some time to really think about what I was trying to do.*
>
> ---**Dr. Kirk**

Establish Your Credibility
Your students should believe that you are the best person to teach your particular class. Establish this on the first day by briefly discussing your professional and academic credentials with your students. Chapters 3 and 4 present specific ways to convince your students that you are an expert in your field.

Stay Current in Your Field
Read journal articles, look over new textbooks, and attend conferences in order to keep current in your subject matter as well as in new teaching methods. Look at local and national newspapers to find examples of applications of the topics you are teaching. Your students will be impressed that you took the time to find timely examples to share with them.

Establish Your Class Culture
You will need to decide how formal, or informal, you want your class to be. This affects everything including how you dress for the classroom, how your students address you, and how you take questions. Will you be Professor or Dr. or will you allow them to call you by your first name? Will you dress professionally or casually? Do students need to raise their hands to ask questions or can they just call them out? It is important to do what feels comfortable to you. However, as mentioned earlier in the book, it is easier to be a little more formal at the beginning and then loosen up than it is to be casual at first and then decide to be strict.

You also get to decide on your attitude each day when you walk into the classroom. You want to be upbeat and enthusiastic so that the students will be excited about the course also. Even if you have had a bad day up until class time, do not let the students know this.

Be Clear About Your Expectations
Set high expectations and communicate these to your students. Ron Theys at the University of Wisconsin-Fond du Lac presents his expectations to his chemistry students by writing them a letter that explains the difference between high school and college classes (see Figure 12.2). He emphasizes that part of what he does is teach them how to learn how to learn.

You might develop a code of conduct for your students or advocate that your college do so for all the students. Salisbury University developed a code of professional and ethical conduct for their business students. Dean William Moore states that the code has been extremely well received by their faculty and students. See Figure 12.3 for a copy of the student code.

Be sure to be consistent in how you treat your students when enforcing your expectations. Your students will be very sensitive to any favoritism they see or perceive. Also, remember the importance of "*withitness.*" As mentioned in Chapter 7, the most effective teachers are aware of what is going on in their classrooms and enforce their policies quickly and fairly.

Relate to Your Students

Relate the course subject matter to your students by taking into account their backgrounds and diverse experiences. You can do this by gathering information the first day from your students as to their majors, jobs or internships, past coursework on the subject, etc. Use a variety of examples and teaching methods in class.

Respect Your Students

Establish a rapport with your students by recognizing them as individuals. Realize that they have other classes, jobs, internships, college organizations, and a personal life to balance. Make sure your assignments are useful and not just "busy work." Show respect for them in how you respond to questions in class. They will be very sensitive to the perception that you believe their questions to be a waste of your time.

> *Are disruptive behaviors linked to extracurricular commitments? Anecdotally, many, many students I've known are spending a lot of time wage-earning, and generally enter the classroom 'distracted'.*
>
> **---John F. Crews**
> **Brown University**

If you need to remind them of your class policies, do so on a one-on-one basis. How you deal with those who break your rules is important. This includes using a matter-of-fact tone of voice and attitude. Getting angry and scolding your students who talk in class will not work as well as just getting quiet, looking at those students, and waiting. Separate your feelings about the student from your feelings about the behavior. The heart of dealing with disruptive behavior is not getting agitated and flustered, but remaining calm. Approach it as, "It is my responsibility to ensure that our classroom is a good place to learn," rather than as, "Why can't you just behave?!" Remember that you are the teacher.

> *Is there such a thing as a stupid question? I once had a student ask me if I kept track of the grades in the class.*
>
> **---Dr. Kirk**

Be Organized
Develop a "to do" list before going into each class for what you want to cover that day. Decide on questions to ask or activities to do. Make notes to yourself as to what homework to give or collect. If you forget that you told the students that there will be a quiz today, and they actually have studied for it, you will have lost some points with them. Do this several times and you start losing their respect.

Undergraduates especially are more comfortable with structure in the classroom. You can achieve this by using overheads, Power Point slides, or lecture outlines. Stop your lecture frequently and summarize. Never lecture for more than 15 minutes at a time, then stop and ask questions of the class or do an activity.

Work on Your Presentation
Work hard on your teaching skills at the begin-

ning of your career so you gain the reputation as a good teacher. Spend time developing good lecture notes with current examples, exercises, and activities. Have a colleague sit in on your class to give you feedback or videotape your class to see what kind of impression you are giving. Attend workshops on teaching to learn from others what works for them in the classroom.

Be a Good Role Model

Be on time to class and demonstrate that you are prepared for every class for the duration of the class. Keep your word; if you tell your students you will do something such as get their exams or papers back on a certain date, then do so.

Learn Names

This shows the students that they are important to you. Use name cards or a seating chart to help you. The seating chart is also useful in taking attendance. Try to learn several names on the first day of class. When a student asks a question, ask for his or her name first and then use it several times when giving your answer.

> *I find it useful to give several short papers the first few weeks that I grade and return to the students. I use the seating chart to put the papers in the order in which the students are seated and then call out their names as I walk down the aisles passing the papers back. This helps me to remember names and where the student sits.*
>
> ---**Dr. Kirk**

Do Not Read to Your Students

One of the comments heard often from students is that they hate it when their professors read the lectures to them. You can prevent this tendency by taking only an in-depth outline to class with you. Use examples that you get from a different textbook on the same subject. The students will not have access to these and will be more interested than if you use the examples that are in their own textbook.

Ask for Feedback

Your university probably has a standard teaching evaluation form but you can also develop your own with questions you would like students to answer. See Figure 12.4 for an example of a written evaluation form. Keep in mind that the tendency is to focus on the few negative comments and ignore the positive ones. If the majority of the students are satisfied with your teaching, then you are doing well. Look at the negative comments to see if there is anything that you should or can change; if not, chalk those up to the fact that you will not be able to please all your students.

Consider asking for feedback at mid-term. If you do so, be sure and respond to the comments you get. Some of the suggestions you may be able to do that semester such as doing a quick review of the last class's notes before beginning a new lecture or giving all the answers to the problems you assign. Others you may have your own reasons for not changing; share these with the students also.

> *I do a quick five-minute review at the beginning of each class. I divide the students up into teams in a different way each day. Sometimes we play the men against the women. Other days I divide the room in half and play the east side of the room against the west side or north against south. I ask questions based on the previous day's lecture and the teams take turns raising their hands to answer without using their notes. I knew the "game" was successful when I came in early to class and found over half of them already there reviewing their notes. There are no points involved but the students like the competition.*
>
> **---Dr. Kirk**

Treat Office Hours as Sacred

Always keep your office hours. If an emergency comes up, be sure to post notice on your office door and indicate when you will be making up those hours.

Never Let Them See You Sweat

Remember perception is reality. To be confident, you have to present yourself as confident. Your students will assume you know your material and if you have done the research and preparation, you will. As they say, there's nothing like teaching a subject to make you really know the content.

> *Being an excellent teacher IS a lot of work. It is more work than being a lousy teacher, no way around it. But it's also far more rewarding, and in my opinion, worth it!*
>
> ---**Paula Thonney,**
> **Brookdale Community College**

What if You Don't Know the Answer?

It is OK to admit occasionally that you do not have the answer to all their questions. Be sure and find out the answer by the next class and share this with them. If it is a "gray area" question, you might make an educated guess based on your experience.

Contingency Plan

Have additional materials, a short case, or a written assignment ready in case you get through the lecture faster than you had planned or the class discussion falls flat. This helps to emphasize that the class time is valuable.

Find a Mentor

Having an experienced and compassionate mentor will help you improve your teaching and deal with students who are misbehaving in your classroom. Talking classroom scenarios out with someone who has been there before will help you to think about things objectively, to remove yourself from the situation emotionally (you can't take it personally!), and to figure out why certain behaviors are unacceptable and what you can do about it. You want to be compassionate but with very high expectations. Also, consider starting or participating in a teaching colloquium at your university where faculty meet on a regular basis to discuss their teaching.

Take Time to Evaluate Your Teaching

Keep a portfolio of your teaching. Make note of any new assignments and approaches you have tried and how these worked. List steps to overcome any problems the students mention in your teaching evaluations. You may be asked to provide information to your chair or dean regarding your teaching to be used in decisions to renew your contract, to give pay raises, or to determine tenure or promotion.

A Final Note

According to Wilbert McKeachie, in his book, *McKeachie's Teaching Tips*, the characteristics that our students want to see from us are:[2]

- Enthusiasm
- A willingness to try to make the course worthwhile
- Objectivity or fairness
- A sympathetic attitude toward the problems of students.

Learning to manage your classroom, and become a more effective teacher, is a craft that can be learned and improved upon like any other skill. The good news is that our students do want us to take control of our classrooms. They appreciate the effort we go through to make the learning experience meaningful.

Most of my classroom management techniques I've developed in response to behavioral problems I've encountered over time. Talking, inattention, multi-tasking, sleeping, tardiness, early departure, mid-lecture restroom breaks, emotional outbursts, inappropriate language, excessive participation and questions, rudeness and profanity, rejection of requirements, whining about grades, demands for reduced workload, insubordination, and outwardly hostile challenges to authority are things for which one has to be prepared. What I have done the last couple of years is tie individual decorum to the participation grade. It's important to reiterate expectations frequently, and to nip transgressions in the bud immediately. I always have to strike a balance in setting the tone, because I feel like a drill sergeant sometimes when I enforce standards. Overall, though, by doing so I have taken back control of my classroom and I have regained the joy of teaching after some early, career threatening management and discipline problems.

---Donald Kent Douglas
Long Beach City College

Figure 12.1: Example of Teaching Philosophy

What I am trying to accomplish in my management classes:

- Help students integrate the knowledge they have already acquired with the concepts, methods, and theories of management. This is done by helping them see relationships between psychology, sociology, political science, history, ethics, philosophy, and literature.

- Give students a sound background and foundation of the history and contributors to management theory in order to help them understand how various theories were developed and tested and why these theories have either been discarded or are still in use today.

- Assist students in acquiring a common management terminology.

- Emphasize the importance of management concepts not only to management majors but to anyone who works with others in organizations.

- Help students develop an understanding of others with different backgrounds, cultures, genders, race, and capabilities, through the use of videos, papers, class discussions, and guest speakers.

- Allow the students to practice both written and oral communication skills and give feedback for improving these.

- Work on developing skills in team building, leadership, motivation, time management, listening, consensus building, creativity, and flexibility.

- Understand the importance and relevance of humor in the classroom and in the workplace.

- Reinforce values of attendance, turning work in on time, treating others with respect, and professionalism in appearance and conduct.

- Provide "real-world" exposure through assignments such as interviewing a manager or working with a company on management-related problems.

In other words, I am trying to create a classroom culture that will challenge, motivate, sometimes even frustrate students, but which allows them to learn not only about management but also about themselves. I believe this is an ongoing process and thus, I am still developing my philosophy of teaching and what it means to be an educated person.

Figure 12.2: Great Expectations

Welcome to Chemistry 145. As college students, there will be many expectations placed upon you and this class will have several expectations of its own. The most important goal is to teach you how to learn on your own, outside the classroom. This is the main feature that distinguishes college from high school. This handout contains expectations that I, as your instructor, have for you, and that you should have for yourself.

The thing you need to realize is that most of you were taught well below the level at which you are capable of learning when you were in high school. This may not seem true to you, but the fact is many of the students who were in high school classes had no college plans and the level of the classes had to suit all of you. This forced the teachers to teach at a level below your capabilities. This is the underlying premise to the facts below, taken from an article written by Steven Zucker, a math professor at Johns Hopkins University.

1. You are no longer in high school. The majority of you will have to discard high school notions of teaching and learning and replace them with university-level notions. This may be difficult, but it has to happen sooner or later, so sooner is better. Our goal is more than getting you to reproduce what was told to you in the classroom.

2. Expect to have material covered at two to three times the pace of high school. Above that, we aim for a greater command of the material, especially the ability to apply what you have learned to new situations when relevant.

3. It is <u>your</u> responsibility to learn the material. Lecture time is at a premium, so it must be used efficiently. You cannot be taught everything in the classroom. Most of the learning must take place outside the classroom. You should expect to put in at least three hours outside the classroom for each hour of class.

4. The instructor's job is to provide a framework to guide you in doing your learning of the concepts and methods that make-up the material of the course. The professor's job is not to program you with isolated facts and problems, nor to monitor your progress.

5. You are expected to read the textbook for comprehension. The text gives the detailed account of the material of the course. It also contains many examples of problems worked out, and should be used to supplement those you see in the lecture. The textbook is not a novel, so the reading must often be slow-going and careful. However, there is the clear advantage that you can read at your own pace.

Source: Ron Theys, University of Wisconsin-Fond du Lac

Figure 12.3: Business Student Code of Professionalism

Faculty at the Perdue School of Business expect every student in business classes to engage in conduct consistent with the professional and ethical conduct a business organization would expect of employees. The norm used in deriving this code of conduct was the general set of behavioral expectations that would apply to a business person while in a meeting with a client and/or a superior. As a guide for students, consider how you would act in such a situation and apply the equivalent standard to your in-class and out-of-class academic interactions.

1. Uphold the highest standards of personal and academic integrity in every facet of the program.
   - Never submit work with the intention of seeking credit for that which was completed by others without fully disclosing and crediting the original author(s) or source.
   - Any form of cheating, illicit collaboration, falsification, or any other act deemed to be in violation of academic integrity standards will result in sanctions in accordance with the University policy, outlined in the Student Handbook.
   - Egregious instances of academic dishonesty can result in dismissal from the business program.

2. Although no dress code is expected, students should not:
- Wear hats in business class or during extra-curricular business school activities.

3. Classes begin and end at set times. Students taking business classes are expected to:
- Be in their seat and ready to begin class at the scheduled time.
  - Arriving late is disruptive and disrespectful.
  - If commuting or parking are concerns, leave for class five-minutes earlier.
- Remain in class until dismissed by the professor.
  - Leaving in the middle of class is unacceptable for non-emergency situations or without prior consent.

4. Students taking business classes are expected to attend all classes.
- Individual faculty members devise thei own attendance policy and absence guidelines.
- Students will be informed of that policy on the first class meeting.

5. While in business classes, students are expected to:
- Turn off all cell phones.
  - If on-call for a legitimate work-related reason, the phone must be set to vibrate.
- Stay awake and alert, with attention focused on the class activity.
  - Sleeping in class will not be tolerated for any reason.
- Refrain from doing anything not related to the

current class (i.e., doing homework for another class; organizing a day planner; reading a newspaper).

- Avoid side conversations.
  - o Talking to a classmate or neighbor during a lecture is disruptive to those students around you who want to learn and disrespectful to the faculty member.

6. When completing assigned coursework, students in business classes are expected to:

- Devote the necessary time outside of class to complete the work.
  - o Expect to spend 2-3 hours per week on coursework for every credit hour earned in the class. For example, a 3-hour business course represents in-class time plus 6-9 hours per week outside-class time.
  - o Students taking a full-time schedule in the business program (15 credit hours per semester) should be dedicating between 30 to 45 hours each week to their courses, not including class time. This is equivalent to what is expected of a full-time employee.
  - o Full-time or part-time employment does not grant students in business classes an exception to the time they are expected to dedicate to their education.
  - o Students choosing to work full or part-time must manage their time carefully so that assignments and projects are

not neglected until the last minute.

- o Students participating in organized campus activities are not exempt from meeting educational expectations in the business program. Course schedules should be planned in advance to avoid any conflict between scheduled activities (e.g., athletic games, performances) and classes.

- Work cooperatively with other students on group assignments.
  - o Respect the need to plan ahead and schedule tasks such that every group member has ample opportunity to meet all of his or her other academic and outside obligations.

In summary, a business person is expected to

- have a presentable appearance;
- arrive on time;
- stay until the meeting or activity concludes;
- be an active, contributing participant during the meeting;
- have the self-control required to remain engaged in the meeting, even when disinterested;
- be prepared, in advance, for the meeting by completing all assigned work; and
- invest the time necessary to complete assignments without passing off another's work as one's own.

Source: William M. Moore, Dean, Franklin P. Perdue School of Business, Salisbury University.

Figure 12.4: Course Evaluation Form

1. What are the major strengths of your professor as a teacher?

2. What could your professor do to improve and become a better teacher?

3. What did you particularly like about this course?

4. What weaknesses do you find in the course as it is set up and what do you propose for eliminating these weaknesses?

Questions from Faculty

Dear Dr. Kirk:
Can you give me your top five tips to help me "take back the classroom?"
Busy With Short Attention Span

Dear Busy,
Establish your credibility; set expectations and be consistent in enforcing them; handle any problems as soon as they occur; keep current on your subject matter; and respect your students. Bonus tip: enjoy teaching! The students can tell if you really want to be there in the classroom.

Dear Dr. Kirk:
In the Chronicle of Higher Education article on September 17, 2004, titled, "Taking Control of the Classroom," Dr. John Drea of Western Illinois University discusses a behavior contract he has students sign the first day of class. Do you think this is a good idea?
Not a Lawyer

Dear Not a Lawyer,
I think it makes sense. A number of professors are beginning to use contracts such as Dr. Drea's that the students are asked to sign stating they will abide by the classroom rules listed on the contract. When issues arise, the professors can hold the student accountable by referring to the contract. When Dr. Drea and his colleagues surveyed their students, they found the majority of them believed the contract was helpful in reducing the number of classroom problems.

Comments from Students

Question: What advice would you give to college professors regarding teaching?

Make class interesting.

Mark

Be prepared for students to be unwilling to give input. Make class interaction and participation mandatory.

Dana

Don't let your class tell you how to grade or let them talk you into lowering standards. I've seen this happen way too often and it takes value away from the class.

Kelly

Keep personal opinions out of classes such as politics and history. Use real world examples. Be relaxed and easy to talk to. Don't feel threatened by students.

Sarah

Don't read to your students-we can read. Use real life examples, it makes it more clear and real to us. We remember these more than random sentences from the book.

Amy

Take control of the class from day one, but don't hesitate to get to know your students. Help them help themselves be successful.

Brad

Involve the class and make it clear how the subject is important to them. Assignments must clearly reflect the material and doing them really assist learning the material. Tests should have applied knowledge questions.

Mary

Be enthusiastic and confident. Don't show fear.
Derek

If you see that a student is performing poorly (i.e. bad grades on tests, papers), try to bring them into your office for help.
Brett

Give timely feedback on presentations and tests.
Pat

Pretend you're in the class with them and together you will fight to understand the material. Otherwise you will be equated with the material (evil and difficult).
Joel

If you are a young and new teacher, realize that we are looking to you for education, not for you to be hip, cool, and our friend. Friendly and approachable is good but there is a line that you should not cross if you want to keep our respect.
Jim

Endnotes:

[1]Montell, Gabriela, "How to Write a Statement of Teaching Philosphy," *Chronicle of Higher Education*, March 27, 2003.

[2]McKeachie, Wilbert J., *McKeachie's Teaching Tips*, 11th Edition, Houghton Mifflin Company, 2002.

APPENDIX

Sample Syllabus

DR. DELANEY J. KIRK
FALL 2005
COURSE SYLLABUS

HUMAN RESOURCE MANAGEMENT (MGMT 182)

Instructor:	Delaney J. Kirk, Ph.D., SPHR Professor of Management
Pre-req of Class:	MGMT 110 or permission of instructor
Office:	Aliber Hall #313
Office Hrs:	Tues. 11-12:30; 3:30-5:30 Thurs 11-12:30; 3:30-5:30 or by appointment
Office Phone:	515-271-3724
E-mail:	delaney.kirk@drake.edu
Web site:	www.cbpa.drake.edu/kirk

Textbook (required)
Mathis, R. and J. Jackson, Human Resource Management: Essential Perspectives, 3rd ed, Thomson/Southwestern Publishing Co., 2005. ISBN #0-324-18341-0

Other Materials
In addition to your textbook, you will be asked to read recent articles in preparation for class discussions and cases. These will be given to you in class.

Brief Course Description
Many of you are either Management majors or other majors who realize the importance of developing management skills. This course introduces the student to the challenges, problems, theories, techniques, opportunities, and social significance of Human Resource Management. Topics will include: EEO laws, recruitment and selection of employees, motivation, safety and health, compensation and benefits, training and development, and diversity.

Learning Objectives
The objective of this course is for students to learn the HR duties of both operating managers and HR specialists and how a Human Resource department adds value to an organization. Students will become familiar with current issues of concern to HR today. By the end of this course, students will:

- Be familiar with the six functional areas of HR Management as developed by the Society for Human Resource Management (SHRM) and the Human Resource Certification Institute (HRCI).
- Know the relevant EEO and other HR-related laws and the Landmark Supreme Court cases that interpret these laws.
- Develop an awareness of how others differ in values, cultures, backgrounds, motivations, and how to manage a diverse workforce.
- Improve critical management skills in decision-making, communication, team building, leadership, creativity, and case analysis in the application of HR concepts to real world scenarios.

Techniques of Instruction
- Lecture
- Class discussion of the text, lecture material, and assigned classic and current articles
- Relevant videos
- Experiential exercises and cases
- Team presentations
- Guest speakers

Examinations
There will be three (3) examinations, including a comprehensive final, and all exams will cover the textbook chapters, assigned readings, lecture notes and class discussion. It is important that you take the exams at the assigned time. If you have to miss an exam, contact the instructor

prior to that class period. Make-up exams must be completed within one week.

Determining Grades
Grading scale for examinations and course work:

Percentage	Grade
90-100	A
80-89	B
70-79	C
60-69	D
below 60	F

Final grades will be based on the following:

Course requirement	Possible Points
Examinations (2)	200
Comprehensive Final	100
Team projects @ 75 pts each (2)	150
Interview of HR Manager	75
Class participation/exercises/cases	25
Total pts possible	550

Major Assignments
Team Projects:
Each team will be assigned two research projects (75 points each possible) and will present these to the class. Approach this from a "what do they need to know" basis and train the class on the topic. Enough written and oral material should be given to your classmates to make them "experts" on the topic. Oral reports will be 30 minutes per team. Team members should be dressed professionally for the formal presentation. Papers to Dr. Kirk should in-

clude an outline of the presentation, in-depth bibliography, and copies of all articles used.

Potential topics:
- Creative recruiting
- Fair Labor Standards Act on overtime pay
- Establishing Employee Assistance Programs (EAP)
- Violence in the workplace
- Complying with the ADA
- Motivating Generation X and Y employees
- Handling employee conflict/complaints
- Doing exit interviews
- Measuring job satisfaction
- How to do wage/salary surveys
- Evaluating training programs
- Implementing a drug testing program
- Selection testing
- Research of web sites and relevant books on HRM
- Casual dress and productivity
- Sexual harassment
- Wellness programs
- Diversity training
- Others with permission of professor

HR Manager Interview:
Your assignment is to interview an HR manager and present your findings in both written form to Professor Kirk and in oral format to the class. The HR manager may be either a generalist or a specialist in a particular HR functional area in a mid-size or large organization. Students cannot use family members for this assignment. In conducting your interview, use the following suggestions:

- How would you define Human Resource Management?
- What are the most critical skills needed to be an effective HR manager? For example, what personal characteristics do you have that make you successful in this field?
- How can a person develop these skills? What is the role of formal education in this process? What do you think is the future demand for job applicants in HR management?
- Describe a normal working day for you. (For example, describe what you did yesterday).
- What are the most critical problems you face as a HR manager?
- What does your company do to motivate your employees?
- If you were to teach a college course on HR management, what topics would you include? How would you actually teach the course?

Include background information on both the HR manager (name, actual job title, educational and work history, work phone #) and the company for which he/she works (type of business, number of employees, unionized/nonunionized, product or service produced, # of employees that directly report to the HR manager, etc.). Papers should contain as much detail as possible including further elaboration of the questions above and additional questions pertaining to topics discussed in class. A written paper including all the above information will be submitted typed, double spaced, and should look as professional as possible (yes, this means a cover sheet). In addition, a short presentation to the class will be given regarding your interview results.

Attendance

Because this is a skills-building course, class attendance and participation is vital. Information will be shared in the class sessions that will impact on the team projects and exams. Excessive absences will have an adverse effect on a student's final grade. You have two "personal days" to use as you wish. More than two absences will be considered excessive and may result in loss of participation points. Contact me at delaney.kirk@drake.edu or 271-3724 if you plan to take a "personal day" and miss class. You are still responsible for turning in any assignments that are due the date of your personal day.

Class Participation

Active participation is expected in this class. A total of 25 points are allocated to participation which will be graded based on:

- your contribution to class discussions and exercises
- relevant questions asked during class
- completion of assigned reaction papers
- working with teammates on projects
- attendance
- general attitude.

Participation will be evaluated by your professor based on both the quality and quantity of your contributions in class.

Equal Opportunity

Drake University does not discriminate on the basis of race, gender, age, disability, veteran status, religion, color, sexual orientation, or national origin. As a representative of Drake, I am committed to maintaining a positive learning environment based on mutual respect, open communication, and non-discrimination.

Please let me know within the first two weeks whether you will need any special consideration due to disabilities or religious holidays in order to participate fully in the class.

Academic Dishonesty

Students who engage in academic dishonesty will receive as a minimum punishment a grade of zero on the assignment or test; more severe punishment may be taken depending upon the circumstances. Any incidents of academic dishonesty will be reported in writing to the Dean of the College as required by the faculty manual. The Dean may choose to pursue additional penalties. Academic dishonesty is defined by Drake University's General Catalog as: "...any activity that seeks to gain credit for work one has not done or to deliberately damage or destroy the work of others. Plagiarism is defined as misrepresenting another's ideas, phrases, discourse or works as one's own. Cheating is defined as the act, or attempted act, of giving or obtaining aid or information by illicit means in meeting any academic requirements, including examinations."

Classroom Policies and Conduct

This course is discussion-based; thus, a relaxed, respectful environment is necessary so that individuals feel free to voice ideas and opinions. Disruptions and disrespectful behavior are damaging to the educational process. Therefore, you are asked to observe the following class policies:

- Display your professionalism by being on time. Do not come to class late or leave early as this unfairly disrupts your colleagues. You will be expected to be in class, seated, and ready to participate at the beginning of the class time. Excessive absences or tardiness will result in loss of participation points.
- You will be expected to spend the entire period in class. Attend to rest room and other needs before class so that you will not have to leave during class time. Exceptions to this rule should be approved by Dr. Kirk prior to the class period.
- Cell phones should be turned off before class.
- You are expected to do your own work for papers, tests, and projects.
- You are expected to contribute your share of work to your team project and to do your best to make the team experience a positive one for all members.
- Value differences in opinion. Confrontation may be created as part of the learning environment, be prepared to leave it in the room and deal with it in a mature fashion.

Late Work
Your work will be considered "late" if it is turned in after the beginning of the class in which it is due. Quizzes and reaction papers will not be accepted late. Major assignments will be penalized by one letter grade per day that it is late. For example, if you turn in an assignment of "A" quality, but turn it in one day late, you would receive no higher than a "B" on the assignment.

Tentative Schedule for MGMT 182

Aug. 23	Intro to HR Management
Aug. 25	Functional Areas of HR Management/Certification (Chap 1)
Aug. 30	Motivation (Chap 2)
Sept. 1	Video: Morris Massey on Values
Sept. 6	Team Building Exercise
Sept. 8	EEO Laws (Chap 3; Appendix C)
Sept. 13	Landmark Supreme Court Cases
Sept. 15	Video on Discrimination
Sept. 20	Workforce Diversity
Sept. 22	Exam #1
Sept. 27	Expertise topics-Teams 1,2
Sept. 29	Expertise topics-Teams 3,4
Oct. 4	Expertise topics-Teams 5,6
Oct. 6	Expertise topics-Teams 7,8
Oct. 11	Job Analysis/Descriptions (Chap 4)
Oct. 13	Recruiting (Chap 5)
Oct. 20	Selection
Oct. 25	Training (Chap 6)
Oct. 27	Guest speakers
Nov. 1	Performance Appraisals (Chap 7)
Nov. 3	HR Interview Paper and Presentation Due
Nov. 8	Compensation (Chap 8)
Nov. 10	Benefits (Chap 9)
Nov. 15	Health & Safety (Chap 10)
Nov. 17	Exam #2
Nov. 22	Expertise topics-Teams 7,8
Nov 29	Expertise topics-Teams 5, 6
Dec. 1	Expertise topics-Teams 3,4
Dec. 6	Expertise topics-Teams 1,2
Dec. 8	Review
Dec. 15	Comprehensive Final

Study Sheet for Final

The following is a list of important laws, terms, and concepts you will be studying this semester. It will be used to develop your comprehensive final. Use this to study from throughout the semester.

A. Laws

Civil Rights Act of 1964, Title VII
Civil Rights Act of 1866
Civil Rights Act of 1871
Age Discrimination in Employment Act
Equal Pay Act of 1963
Davis-Bacon Act of 1931
Walsh-Healey Act of 1936
Executive Order 11246
Executive Order 10988
Vocational Rehabilitation Act of 1973
Occupational Safety and Health Act of 1970
Fair Labor Standards Act of 1938
Social Security Act of 1935
Pregnancy Discrimination Act of 1978
Immigration Reform and Control Act-1986
Americans with Disabilities Act of 1990
Civil Rights Act of 1991
Family & Medical Leave Act of 1993
Uniformed Services Employment Rights Act

B. Supreme Court Decisions
> Griggs v. Duke Power Co. (1971)
> McDonnell-Douglas Corp v. Green (1973)
> Meritor Savings Bank v. Vinson (1986)
> Johnson v. Transportation Agency (1987)
> United States v. Paradise (1987)

C. Theories
> Equity Theory
> Expectancy Theory
> Motivation Theories

D. Terms
> Adverse Impact
> Disparate Treatment
> Affirmative Action
> Validity/Reliability
> 4/5's Rule
> Job analysis
> Job description
> Job specifications
> Comparable Worth
> Job/Position
> SHRM
> Exempt v. Nonexempt ees
> Job evaluation/methods
> Benefits/types/history of
> BFOQ
> 6 Functional areas of P/HRM
> Accreditation programs in P/HRM

What I Hope You Take From This Book

- Establish credibility the first day of class. Share your background, academic credentials, industry experience, and illustrate why you are the best person to teach this class.

- Set expectations and be consistent in enforcing them. If attendance is important, then tell the students this and reward for regular attendance. If you want assignments turned in on time, then either don't accept late papers or take off points if they are late. Whatever you do, be consistent.

- Handle discipline problems as soon as they happen. If a student is coming in tardy and you do not address the problem, he or she will not all of a sudden decide to come to class on time. If you do not say anything, you have essentially rewarded the wrong behavior.

- Show the students that your knowledge is up-to-date and will benefit them in the long run. Bring in current research studies, newspaper articles, or other examples related to the course topics.

- Show students that you care about them as people: learn names, and create a classroom culture where they can feel comfortable asking questions.

About the Author

Delaney J. Kirk, Ph.D., SPHR, is a tenured professor of management at Drake University with 25 years of teaching experience (learned the hard way sometimes) in both large and small, public and private universities. Dr. Kirk has conducted teaching workshops at a number of universities and professional conferences. She teaches several three-day workshops on classroom management each summer as part of the National Science Foundation's Chautauqua program for college professors. She was the featured expert for the *Chronicle of Higher Education's* online chat on classroom management on September 15, 2004, and has earned the prestigious Drake University Board of Governor's "Excellence in Teaching" Award. She is currently working on another book on teaching which is slated for publication in Summer 2006.

Please feel free to contact Dr. Kirk with your own stories and suggestions on class management at: delaney.kirk@drake.edu. She is also available for workshops at your university or conference.